CW01618813

YOUNG MASTER SERIE

# THE 11+ BRIDGE BOOK

**YOUNG MASTER SERIES**

# THE 11+ BRIDGE BOOK

ALAN & MAUREEN HIRON

Illustrations by E.H.HANDFORTH

THE CROWOOD PRESS

Published by
The Crowood Press,
Crowood House, Ramsbury,
Marlborough, Wiltshire,
SN8 2HE, England,



British Library Cataloguing in Publication Data

Hiron, Alan
The 11+ bridge book. – (Young master series)
1. Contract bridge – Juvenile literature
I. Title II. Series
795.41'5 GV1282.3

ISBN Hardback 0-946284-10-5
Softback 0-946284-15-6

Photoset by Inforum Ltd, Portsmouth
Printed in Great Britain

# CONTENTS

# PREFACE

Bridge-players, like policemen, are getting younger every year. Some fifteen years ago the English Bridge Union, suspecting that there might be some mild interest, started a school's competition.

The response was extraordinary and the size of the event increased year by year. Nowadays there are local leagues, knock-out competitions, pairs events, junior international matches – practically everything that is available in the senior bridge world.

Most of the schools' players are from fifth and sixth forms, but there have been some notable exceptions. Indeed, we have known a nine-year-old who played a perfectly sensible game!

Some people might say that students should be studying and not wasting their time playing games but it doesn't work out like that. Bridge, like chess, makes its players think logically and this is excellent training for practically every other more academic pursuit.

"HARRIS, ANOTHER BOTTLE OF THE '29 I THINK."
'29

# Chapter 1

## THE TOOLS OF THE TRADE

Once you have decided that you want to learn to play bridge you will ask "What equipment will I need?" The answer is simple – the very minimum is a pack of cards and three other players. Of course, you can go in for luxuries like a card-table and four chairs, score-pads, a spare pack of cards and all the rest of it, but they are not *essential.*

I have played bridge in a windy field, an aeroplane, a punt (one of the cartoons shows what actually happened to me) and in a car where the driver actually let the windscreen mist up so that he could write his hand down – this is not recommended!

One thing is certain – you don't have to buy any protective clothing or anything expensive. It has been suggested that a batsman's protective headgear is a good idea when playing with some partners, but that was perhaps not too serious a suggestion. You note the word *partner*? Yes, bridge is completely a partnership game for four players. When writing it is very convenient to refer to the four players round the table as:

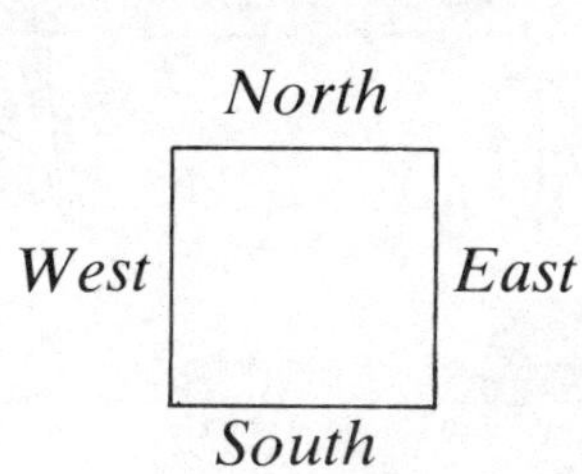

This doesn't mean that you have to wear a little label "East" hung round your neck before you can sit down and play; it simply saves the writer from saying "The player whose cards are written down at the top of the page," when in one word he can say "North". Not surprisingly, the pairs of players facing each other are partners. If North does something good and collects a lot of points for the score sheet, his partner (South) benefits just as much. By contrast, if West does something foolish and loses a lot of points unnecessarily, then his partner (East) suffers in the same way.

It is this factor that has given bridge the reputation of being a quarrelsome game. It has led to at least two murder cases where one of a partnership had not quite seen eye to eye with the other's ideas. Don't worry, the victims really had done horrible things – nothing like that will ever happen to you if you read this book carefully.

Just suppose that you can go beyond one pack of cards and an upturned soap-box. . . . A card table, covered with baize or a cloth is a big improvement on a polished surface when cards go skidding off the edge in an irritating way. Chairs help, of course, and most households have them. You will find it awkward, though, if you start off with deep reclining chairs and have to hoist yourself up before you can see the top of the table.

Another luxury I mentioned was the idea of using two packs of cards. Not at the same time, mind you! The idea is simply for one player to be shuffling one pack for the next hand while another one is dealing the present hand. It saves time and (as you will see) serves to remind you whose turn it is to deal next.

Each pack of cards that you use is an absolutely standard pack of fifty-two. Be warned, you don't want the two jokers that you will find in most new packs. On the other hand, you may not be popular if you tear them up for a number of other card games do need them. Keep them in the box.

Scorepads? Another luxury. They are helpful, for all four players normally keep the score. If someone gives you some, be thankful, but it is not at all difficult to score on any old scrap of paper. When I learnt to play we used a cheap plastic-topped table. We scored on the surface in pencil and used a damp cloth to rub it out at the end of the session.

# Chapter 2

## DO YOU PLAY WHIST?

(If so, skim through this chapter.)

As already suggested, we find ourselves with four would-be players and (at least one) pack of cards. It is no good looking at a pack of cards – they don't do anything by themselves and somebody has to *deal* them. To decide who this is going to be, the cards are spread across the table (face downwards, of course) and each of the four players draws one card and turns it face up. It is the highest card that tells you who is to deal. Yes, I can hear you asking two questions. (1) Does an Ace count high or low? In bridge, as in whist, the Ace is always a high card and the rest run in the natural order – King, Queen, Jack, (or Knave) ten, nine, eight, seven, six, five, four, three, two. (2) What happens if two players draw the same card, for example, they both pull out an Ace? In bridge, the suits have an order of importance – a ranking order – and this is something that you really do have to remember as it comes up later in the game. At the top – spades, then hearts, diamonds and clubs. So in the cut the Ace of Hearts will come behind the Ace of Spades, but will outrank the other two Aces. If you find it difficult to remember (and it is important), you can always fall back on the idea that they are in reverse alphabetical order, (S.H.D.C.).

Fine, now you know who has won the cut. They have a number of privileges. First, they can choose whether they would like to deal with the pack with the red backs or the black backs (or the blue or the green – whatever two different packs you are using). You may think that it doesn't really matter, and you would be quite right – it doesn't. But unless you *say* which pack you want to deal, your opponents won't know which one to shuffle for you. Secondly, the winner of the cut can choose his seat. Thirdly, once you have chosen your seat, the player who has drawn the second highest card comes round to face you as your partner. After that, your opponents, who have drawn the two lowest cards, make their own arrangements. Complicated? Not really, and it does save any arguments.

You may consider that it is enough to have chosen your seats and decided who is to deal. Not quite – there is still a bit of ritual to be enacted before things start. Remember you have chosen, say, the red pack of cards when you won the cut. The player on your left now shuffles the red pack. (There are many ways of shuffling cards, but any way that mixes them up sensibly is good enough. If you feel clumsy when you try it, then practise doing it on your own.) You pick up the shuffled pack and slide it across to the player on your right, saying (to be polite) "Cut, please". He takes the top half of the pack and puts it down nearer to you. You pick up the remaining cards and place them on top before you start to deal. The idea of the cut is to prevent anyone seeing the bottom card! Which will end up with the dealer for the cards are dealt one at a time, clockwise, starting with the player on the dealer's left. Remember, the full pack of fifty-two cards is used, so everybody ends up with thirteen cards. If you are superstitious, now is the time to get over it, for every bridge hand that you will ever be dealt will contain thirteen cards. Everyone picks up their hand, taking care to let no-one else see the faces of their cards, and – very sensibly – sorts them into suits.

Apart from the deal, when a hand of bridge is played, there are two distinct stages:

(1) The *bidding* (or 'auction')
(2) The play of the cards

Although this is the order in which things happen at the table in a real-life game, it is impossible for you to have any idea about the bidding until you have got the idea of the play clearly in mind. So, what is the play all about?

The sequence of events is as follows: one of the four players (and it will only be later on that we find out which of the four it is) takes a card from his hand and puts it face up in the middle of the table. The other three players in turn, clockwise round the table, each contribute a card to the table centre. When all four have played the little pile of cards constitutes a *trick*.

There are several points to note:

(1) The player who plays the highest card in the suit led wins the trick.
(2) Once a card has been led, the other three players *must* follow suit if they can. If they have no more cards in the suit that has been led, they must throw away a card from some other suit, with no chance of winning the trick.

For example:

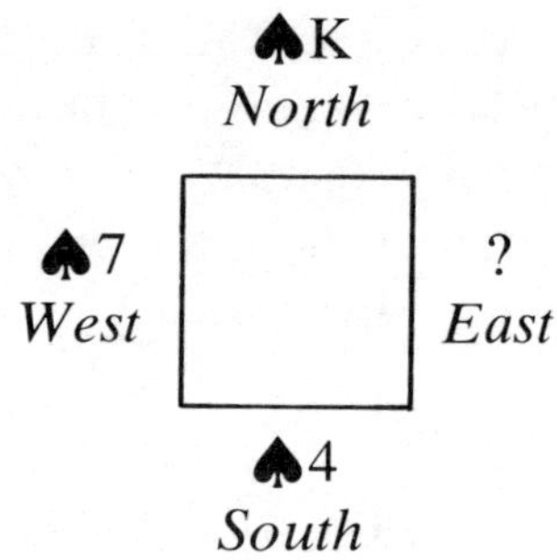


If East's card is the Ace of spades he will win the trick. But if, with no spades left in his hand, he plays the Ace of Hearts it will be North who wins the trick – he has contributed the highest card in the suit that was led.

(3) It doesn't matter whether you or your partner win the trick – it simply counts for your side. So even if South had held ♠A he wouldn't have played it. Instead he would let his partner's King win and save the Ace in the hope of making another trick later. At all times you and your partner are interested in making as many tricks as possible. Everyone has started with thirteen cards, so on every hand there are thirteen tricks at stake. You beat the opponents 13–0, marvellous, a Grand Slam, but it doesn't happen all that often. Far more likely is that the hand will prove a grim fight with perhaps seven tricks going to one side and six to the other.

(4) The player who wins the trick is the one who leads to the next trick.

If you have got your four players, now is the time to try things out. Cut, shuffle and deal as suggested and let the player on the left of the dealer make the opening lead to start things off. Do this a few times – get the feel of taking tricks. Remember that you are not fighting against your partner. If he has won the first trick and you win the second, don't start two separate piles of tricks made, keep them all in one place. It is a good idea to stock them like this:

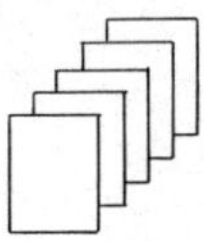

or

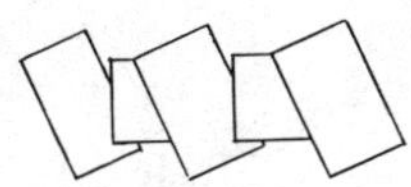

so at the end of the hand it is easy to count how many tricks your side has made.

Fine, you have got the feeling of making tricks, but you are still not quite playing whist. There is another important idea that has to be introduced – the idea of *trumps*.

This is what it is all about – before each hand is played, one of the four suits is given a special part to play – it is chosen as trumps and the cards in that suit become all important. Suppose that diamonds are selected as trumps and that, starting with West, a trick goes as follows:

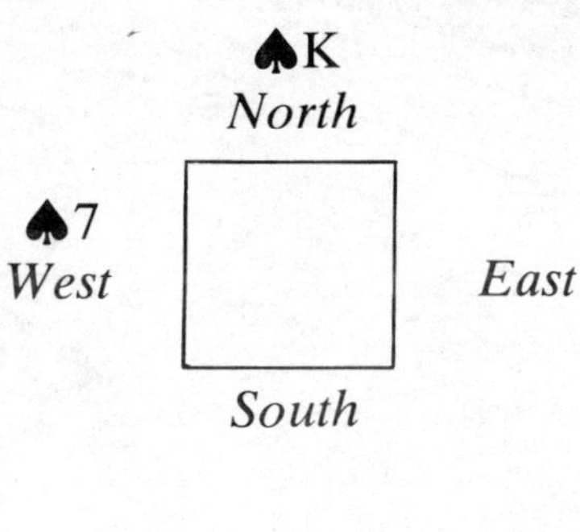

"WHOSE DEAL IS IT?"
DANGER – WEIR

Last time we looked at this trick East played the Ace of spades and won. But suppose that he hasn't got any spades left? Normally he has no choice other than to discard something from another suit with no chance of winning the trick. But if diamonds are trumps he can put on even the two of diamonds and win the trick. The trumps are all-important master cards, but they may only be played if you haven't got any cards left in the suit led.

Can you see how, even if East is able to trump with ♢2, he may still not win the trick? I expect that you have got there – South, just like East, has no more spades (the suit that has been led) and is able to play a higher trump (overtrumping, as we say) and so win the trick. Of course, he doesn't *have* to overtrump, he can throw away a card in another suit, as before. But you must remember that you are in the business of trying to *win* tricks, and although there may be exceptions, it often pays to take whatever is presented.

As well as choosing one of the four suits as a trump suit, a hand may also be played in *no-trumps* where, quite simply, there is no trump suit, and every trick is won on merit.

If you have never played whist (or any of a dozen or so card games involving tricks) it is an excellent idea to deal out a number of hands, playing them in sets of five with clubs, diamonds, hearts and spades as trumps in turn, then one in no-trumps.

Remember the points I have made – it is a *partnership* game and you are trying to make as many tricks for your *side* as possible.

We talk much more about this later on, but just because you have been dealt an Ace there is no panic to win a trick with it. If you *lead* an Ace, you usually collect a two and a three belonging to your opponents. Wouldn't it be more satisfactory to wait a little, still win the trick and kill off a King or a Queen belonging to the other side?

# Chapter 3

## WHAT A BID MEANS AND WHEN YOU OPEN THE BIDDING

In whist or solo, the trump suit for any particular hand is chosen in a very simple way. The dealer turns over his last card and says, "Ah! Hearts are trumps!" and so the hand is played. Sometimes a spare pack of cards is cut to decide what will be trumps. In bridge the selection of trumps is very much more sophisticated, and a great deal more fun. Do you remember from the last chapter the two stages of each hand?

(1) The bidding (or auction)
(2) The play

We have talked about the play and we know what "tricks" and "trumps" mean, so now we are in a position to consider the bidding.

Just suppose that you have dealt yourself your standard ration of thirteen cards and that your hand contains more cards in spades than any other suit. If you were asked which suit you would like to have as trumps, the answer is easy – spades. In whist it would be sheer luck whether spades became trumps or not, but now you have a chance to have a say in the matter. As well as plenty of spades let us imagine that you have a good ration of high cards (Aces, Kings, Queens . . .) that are likely to win tricks. As the dealer you have the chance to make the first *bid* and your obvious idea will be to suggest spades as trumps. After all, you have more cards in spades than any other suit and you are always hoping to make as many tricks as possible.

What do you say then? "I want to play with spades as trumps!" Hardly, for there are three other players at the table and they may also have opinions of their own. Instead you say the words "One Spade".

*One* Spade? I can hear you asking – do you mean taking only one trick with spades as trumps? That would be all too easy if only you had been dealt the Ace of spades! No, when a player bids "One Spade", what he is suggesting is that, *with his partner's co-operation*, his side can take one **plus six** out of the thirteen tricks with the advantage of choosing spades as trumps. You **always** have to add on six to what you bid to appreciate the number of tricks that your side hopes to make. For example, a bid of "Two Hearts" means "I think partner and I can make at least 6 + 2 = 8 tricks if we are allowed to play the hand with hearts as trumps".

"Five Diamonds" means "I think partner and I can make at least 6 + 5 = 11 tricks if we are allowed to play the hand with diamonds as trumps", and so on.

Of course, you may have been dealt a bad hand (I usually am!) with perhaps a Queen and an odd Jack with which to do battle. If you think that you still have to tell the world about your best suit (or to be more accurate, your least bad suit) then don't worry. Instead you say "No Bid" – in other words you are not prepared to join in the bidding at the moment.

Sometimes you will hear players saying "Pass", which is

just another way of saying "No Bid." In this country "No Bid" is more common – if you intend to play some of your bridge in America, then get used to drawling "Pass". The *rules* of bridge, fortunately, are completely international.

(While talking about alternative words, you will sometimes hear someone say "I should have ruffed the second club!" Ruffed? No, not another new idea. To ruff is exactly the same as to trump. Both words come from a very old card game called Triumph – an ancestor of whist – and you can see how the name bent itself into "trump" and "ruff" over the centuries.)

As I stressed before, everything in bridge runs clockwise. If South had opened the bidding with "One Spade" it would now be West's turn to do something. He could say "No Bid" or he could take some action. Suppose that he didn't have a bad hand either and wanted to suggest hearts as trumps? Remember that we also called the bidding stage "The Auction." Well, I expect that you have been to an auction sale. If somebody else bids £100 for a painting it is no use you offering £50 or even £100 again. If you want to make a bid then it has got to be a higher one than the last. In other words, "Two Hearts" to get past "One Spade". Now North, (the third player round the table) would like to show his diamonds. Fine, but it has got to be a bid of "Three Diamonds" before he gets past "Two Hearts". And if he is not prepared to commit his side to trying for nine tricks with diamonds as trumps, then he must say "No Bid".

This goes on, round and round the table, until the four players have run out of breath and/or enthusiasm. The bidding in fact stops when three players in succession say "No Bid". That is very reasonable – after all, you don't bid against yourself in an auction sale – and if the bidding has gone:

| *SOUTH* | *WEST* | *NORTH* | *EAST* |
|---|---|---|---|
| 1 ♠ | 2 ♡ | 3 ◇ | No Bid |
| No Bid | No Bid | | |

then everything is over. With diamonds as their chosen trump suit the North-South partnership will attempt to make at least nine tricks out of the thirteen. (Six as usual, plus the three that they have bid.)

It is only when we start talking about the scoring that we get the idea that, in general, it doesn't pay to bid too enthusiastically. True, you may have a lot of clubs but if your side hasn't got very much in the way of high cards it can prove more expensive in the long run to fail by several tricks than to let the opponents make their own contract. In principle, you only bid whatever you think that you and your partner have a reasonable chance of making.

One thing is certain – if the bidding always advances One something, Two something, Three something and so on, it is going to get very high very quickly.

Do you remember when we talked about cutting the cards we decided that the four suits had an order or importance – a ranking order – with spades at the top, then hearts, then diamonds and finally clubs? (Alphabetical order, if you forget.)

This order applies in the bidding as well. If South has opened the bidding with "One Club" and West (the next player to speak) wants to bid diamonds, he can say "One Diamond" – a higher ranking suit than clubs, and so a higher bid. Indeed the bidding could start:

| *SOUTH* | *WEST* | *NORTH* | *EAST* |
|---|---|---|---|
| 1♣ | 1♢ | 1♡ | 1♠ |

But if South, at his second turn wants to bid clubs again, he would have to bid "Two Clubs" to get past East's last bid of "One Spade".

You can think of all the possible bids arranged as a ladder: 1♣, 1♢, 1♡, 1♠, 2♣, 2♢, 2♡, 2♠, 3♣, 3♢, . . . . . . 7♡, 7♠, with 1♣ as the bottom rung and 7♠ as the top one. And once a bid has been made, all later bids must come from higher up the ladder. You can see the importance of remembering the order of the suits!

There is another important idea that you will have already met if you play whist. As well as choosing any of the four suits as trumps, you can suggest that you would like the hand to be played without any trumps at all – in other words, all of the tricks will be won on merit. If you haven't got a card in the suit led, then you have no choice but to throw away a card from another suit with no chance of winning the trick. This is called *discarding*. You try to play without trumps (usually when you have an all-round hand with no long suit, but much more of that later) by bidding "No-trumps" in just the same way that you would bid a suit. And in the bidding, no-trumps rank as the highest of all. So, if someone has bid "One Spade" you can make a call of "One No-trump." As usual, this means that you hope your partnership can win at least seven tricks, but now, of course, without the help of any trumps.

We shall have to re-arrange the ladder of all possible bids, now: 1♣, 1♢, 1♡, 1♠, 1NT, 2♣, 2♢, 2♡, 2♠, 2NT, 3♣, . . . . . . 7♡, 7♠, 7NT.

So far we have *talked* a lot about bridge hands. It is time that you looked at one. A hand is always *written* like this:

| | |
|---|---|
| SPADES | ♠A K 7 6 4 |
| HEARTS | ♡K Q 5 2 |
| DIAMONDS | ♢2 |
| CLUBS | ♣A J 9 |

Do you get the idea? Always spades first, then hearts, diamonds and clubs.

Next problem. Would you describe this hand as a good hand or a bad hand? Certainly it has got a fair number of high cards but it would be a help if we could count them in some way. The simplest and best idea is the *point-count*. For every Ace that you hold – count 4 points; for every King – 3 points; for every Queen – 2 points; and for every Jack – 1 point.

So, if you take the hand that we have just looked at:

| | | |
|---|---|---|
| ♠A K 7 6 4 | = | 7 points |
| ♡K Q 5 2 | = | 5 points |
| ♢2 | = | 0 points |
| ♣A J 9 | = | 5 points |
| Total | = | 17 points |

It is worth doing a little arithmetic. In each suit there are ten possible points; there are four suits, so the pack contains 40 points; there are four players; and so the *average* hand has 10 points. Now, if you have only an average hand, why should your side do better than your opponents?

It is good, sensible advice to open the bidding only when you have a better than average hand – 13 points or more. It is an easy number to remember as it is the same number of cards that you hold.

Is that all? Not quite – just look at these two hands:

| (a) | | (b) | |
|---|---|---|---|
| | ♠7 | | ♠7 6 3 |
| | ♡A 9 8 7 6 3 | | ♡A 9 8 7 |
| | ◇5 | | ◇6 5 4 |
| | ♣A K 8 6 4 | | ♣A K 8 |

Well, both hands have eleven points and are apparently not quite worth an opening bid but which of the two hands would you prefer to be dealt? Yes, quite right – hand *(a)*. After all, if you are going to suggest your longest suit (hearts) as trumps it must be better to have a six-card suit rather than only a four-card suit. Length in trumps produces tricks. A simple way of adjusting the value of a hand to take account of a long suit is as follows:

With a *five*-card suit add *one* extra point to your total.
With a *six*-card suit add *two* extra points to your total.

Don't take the idea too far – for example, if you are dealt all thirteen cards in a suit it is hardly worth while working out how many points you have got for you are looking at thirteen sure tricks if only you can make your suit trumps.

Good, so now you can value any hand that you are dealt. It is a good idea to practice quietly on your own – dealing a number of hands and getting into the habit of counting your points quickly so that when you play with others you don't hold things up too much.

"SINCE YOU HAPPEN TO MENTION IT, I SUPPOSE I COULD HAVE PLAYED THE HAND DIFFERENTLY."

# Chapter 4

## WHAT DO YOU CHOOSE FOR YOUR BID?

Having decided that you need 13 or more points to start things off, the question is, which suit would you prefer as trumps? Suppose that you had dealt yourself

♠A K J
♡J 9 6 5 2
◇A 8 3
♣J 7

Would you open One Spade or One Heart? The spades are powerful, but only three in number, the hearts are much weaker, but there are five.

Almost without exception you should bid your *longest suit first*. Your top spades are likely to win tricks whatever are trumps. Your hearts are only likely to play any part in the proceedings if they are trumps. True, the high ones are missing but if the other eight cards in the suit are shared fairly evenly round the table, you will have two more than anyone else, and two extra trumps are always two tricks.

*Note well that you do not make an opening bid in a suit with fewer than four cards.*

You are now in a position to make a sensible opening bid on most hands that you will ever be dealt! With less than 13 points, pass; with 13 or more, bid one of your long suit. Only most hands, though, for there are still one or two possible problems. For example, look at this hand:

♠A K J 3
♡5 4 2
◇7 3
♣A K J 3

Sixteen points, so it is an opening bid, but you have two suits of the same length. Should you open One Spade or One Club? Try it out. Suppose that after you have bid your partner wants to tell you about a diamond suit that he has got. As you don't think much of the idea of playing the hand with diamonds as trumps, it seems sensible to tell partner about your other suit.

| | *SOUTH* | *WEST* | *NORTH* | *EAST* |
|---|---|---|---|---|
| (a) | 1 ♠ | No Bid | 2 ◇ | No Bid |
| | 3 ♣ | | | |

| | *SOUTH* | *WEST* | *NORTH* | *EAST* |
|---|---|---|---|---|
| (b) | 1 ♣ | No Bid | 1 ◇ | No Bid |
| | 1 ♠ | | | |

You can see the difference: (b) is correct as both suits are shown at the one level, (a) works badly as you are already committed to trying for nine tricks and you may still not have found a suit that both you and your partner like.

In this example, bidding the lower ranking suit first worked better, but it doesn't always pan out like that. When you start with two suits of the same length, everything depends on whether they are next to each other in the ranking order, or whether there is at least one missing suit in between. The neighbouring pairs are spades/hearts; hearts/diamonds; diamonds/clubs. With one of these hands you do better to open the bidding with one of the higher ranking suit. So with:

♠A K J 3
♡A K J 3
♢7 5
♣5 4 2

Open One Spade, not One Heart. It is not quite so clear why this works out better, but we will come back to that later. For the moment, just get into the habit of sticking to the two rules suggested.

Now you have even more scope for practice without partner or opponents. Deal four hands and, one at a time, count the points and decide on an opening bid.

Next, look at these two hands:

| (a) | | (b) | |
|---|---|---|---|
| | ♠A Q 4 | | ♠K J 5 |
| | ♡none | | ♡A 10 7 |
| | ♢A K Q J 9 7 | | ♢Q 7 4 2 |
| | ♣A K 6 3 | | ♣K J 2 |

What have they got in common? Two things, I suppose. They are both opening bids and in both cases diamonds is the longest suit. But that is where the similarity ends. Hand (a) has a long suit and a *void*, (no cards in a suit), and it is obvious that you would insist on diamonds as trumps. It is quite certain that you wouldn't want to play in no-trumps, for if you did, your opponents might be able to take five or six heart tricks before you ever get in. Remember the idea of no-trumps? You would be helpless.

Hand (b), however is what we call a *balanced hand*. The diamond suit is nothing to write home about and you have your high cards well shared out over the four suits. This makes it an ideal hand on which to suggest the idea of playing in no-trumps as soon as possible.

It is worth noting that you have enough "stuffing" in each suit to provide a *guard* or a *stopper*. The Ace is always enough to stop the opponents from taking all of the tricks in a suit, the King is enough too – but of course it now needs to be protected with at least one other card in the same suit. For example, if you hold K 2 in a suit, your opponents can take the Ace, but then your King is the master. In the same way, a Queen can produce a stopper, but only if it is backed up with at least two low cards. The other side take their Ace and King (to which you follow with low cards) and you have the Queen left as a winner. Even the Jack can be a guard – try working out how!

At least you now have a good idea of the type of hand that wants to suggest no-trumps – balanced, with high cards well shared out. In fact, there is quite a strong incentive to play in no-trumps if both your hand and your partner's hand are suitable. It all hinges on the scoring, and although you would find a full table of bridge scoring a complete waste of time at this stage, it will be helpful to get some picture of what the objects of the game are. Perhaps you think that I have been putting the cart before the horse, but until you have a working knowledge of tricks, trumps, and what a bid means, it is difficult to get any further.

Right, when you sit down to play, your object in life for the next half-hour or so, is to win the *rubber*. The rubber is won by the side that first bids and makes two *games*. It is very much like a three set match in tennis. If you win the first two sets it is all over but, if you get to one set all, you have to play a decider. Just the same in bridge – two consecutive games and the rubber is finished – one game all and you play on.

You can only achieve a game by *bidding and making* contracts that give you 100 points on the score sheet. (It is unfortunate that we use the word "points" in more than one sense. We have used points to value our hand but these points are simply a help to the player. Now we are talking about the points that go down on the score sheet.) You don't have to do everything in one go, you can build up your 100 points with more than one bite at the cherry.

The suits score as follows:

For every spade or heart that you *bid and make* you score *30 points*. (The *major* suits.)
For every diamond or club that you *bid and make* you score *20 points*. (The *minor* suits.)

The score sheet looks like this:

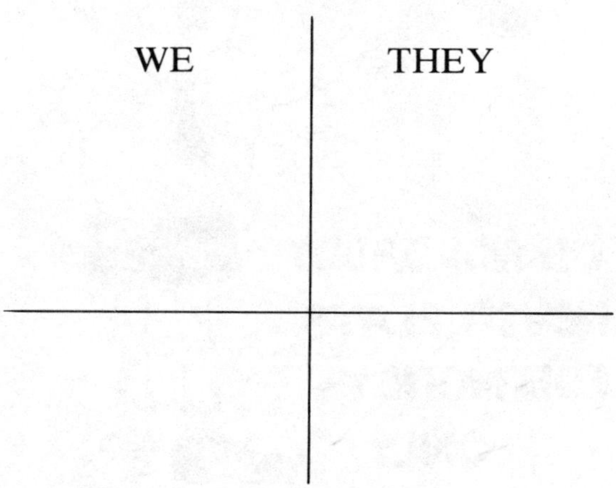

"OH NO! DADDY NEVER PLAYS FOR MONEY - ONLY FRIENDLIES."

and "WE" and "THEY" are self descriptive. Don't forget, it is normal for everyone to score, so at the end of the rubber your score card and your partner's should look alike and the cards of both opponents should be a mirror image of yours.

Now, there are two places where you can score for your side – above the line and below the line. The important place is *below the line* for that is where you record the points for contracts that you have both *bid and made*. This cannot be stressed too much; it is no good bidding a contract if you don't make it (you score nothing at all!). And you don't get the full benefit from making tricks that you *have not* bid. (You collect something from them but the points only go above the line, and don't count towards a game.)

Let's score a possible rubber on the blank diagram:

*Hand 1.* You and your partner bid Two Spades and make nine tricks. You score 60 points below the line (*bid and made* at 30 points per trick) and 30 points above the line. Useful, but as you hadn't bid it, these points do not count towards your game. (If you had bid One Spade and made nine tricks, you would have scored 30 below the line – counting towards game – and 60 above the line. If you had bid Three Spades and made nine tricks, all 90 of your points would have gone below the line.)

*Hand 2.* Your opponents bid Two Diamonds and made nine tricks. What do they score? Right, you've got the idea now – they score 40 points below the line and 20 above for the *overtrick* that they collected.

If you have filled in your score sheet, it should now look like this:

| WE | THEY |
|---|---|
| 30 | 20 |
| 60 | 40 |

Both sides have made what we call a *part-score*. (This really does explain itself!)

*Hand 3.* You and your partner have bid and made a contract of Two Clubs. Easy, you say, I know how to score that – 40 points below the line. But something special has happened – you have built up 100 points below the line, and that makes a game. You celebrate this by drawing a line across *both* columns and now the score looks like this:

| WE | THEY |
|---|---|
| 30 | 20 |
| 60 | 40 |
| 40 | |

Your opponents' 40 part-score has been chopped off. Again, think of tennis – if you win the first set 6–4, you don't let the opponent carry forward the four games that he has scored to give him a start in the next set! So it is in bridge – they will still get the credit for those 40 points below the line that they have earned but, as regards trying to build up to the 100 points that they need for game, they will have to start again from scratch.

*Hand 4.* Your opponents, perhaps annoyed that you have made a game, bid a contract of Four Hearts and make eleven tricks. (120 below the line, draw a line, 30 above.) The position is now that both sides have made a game – *game all*, or both sides *vulnerable*. The word vulnerable is often used to describe a partnership who have made one game, but have not yet clinched the rubber. Later on we will see that this can affect the scoring for *undertricks*. (When you fail to make your contract.)

*Hand 5.* The game in one blow gets your opposition excited and they try the same thing again on the next hand. They bid Five Clubs (which score them 100 points if they make it) but things go badly for them and they end up with only nine tricks. They didn't make their contract, they score nothing, you collect! In fact, you pick up 200 points (*above* the line, of course, because you didn't bid and make anything) and the rubber proceeds. (Fill in the score!)

*Hand 6.* Against slightly demoralised opponents, you and your partner bid and make four spades. That gives you your second game and the rubber. You have, in fact, won the rubber by two games to one and that gives you a bonus of 500 points. Strictly speaking, this goes above the line but as the rubber is over it doesn't really matter where you write it, because the time for adding up has come. If you had been lucky (or skilful!) enough to win the rubber by two games to nil, you would have collected the larger bonus of 700 points.

Now you can see the importance of trying to bid and make *games* – if you can build up two before the other side, you get a substantial addition to your score.

I hope, too, that you are starting to get a glimmering of an idea of what bidding is all about. Not only do you and your partner want to find out which of the four suits (or no-trumps) appeals to you both the most, but also you want to try and judge whether your partnership has the values to bid a game.

The problems then: Which suit? How high?

But more of that later.

Did you finish scoring the rubber that you have just played? It should look like the score sheet on page 39.

All over, and if you had arranged to play for 1p per hundred points, this would mean that you would triumphantly collect 7p from an opponent and your partner would collect the same amount from the other one. But that would

| WE | THEY |
|---|---|
| 500 | |
| 200 | 30 |
| 30 | 20 |
| 60 | 40 |
| 40 | |
| | 120 |
| 120 | |
| TOTAL | TOTAL |
| 950 | 210 |

*Difference – 740 points*

be after three-quarters of an hour's hard work. So don't regard stakes of 1p per hundred as heavy gambling! And yet, you know, it is a funny thing that even playing for tiny stakes gives you a sense of responsibility. If you play for nothing, what is to stop you playing every hand? Going off most of the time, yes, but having all the fun. . . .

Now that we have an idea of the scoring, we can come back briefly to the idea of bidding no-trumps. Nothing has been said so far about what no-trump contracts score. The answer is a tiny bit odd (like so many things in bridge).

No-trumps, in principle, score the same as the major suits (30 points per trick). But the first one in any no-trump contract that is bid and made scores 10 extra points.

A contract of 1NT, bid and made, scores 40 points.

A contract of 2NT, bid and made, scores 40 + 30 = 70 points.

A contract of 3NT, bid and made scores 40 + 30 + 30 = *100 points*.

Are you there? *Three no-trumps*, only nine tricks, give you game if you make it, whereas you need ten tricks to clock up a major suit game, and eleven for a minor suit game. Nine tricks are easier than ten, and much easier than eleven. Now, at last, you can see the incentive for you and partner to play in a no-trump contract *if your hands are suitable*. It doesn't make sense to fail by a lot of tricks in the wrong contract if you could have made something sensible (even if you had scored slightly less).

Come back to the no-trump hand that we had considered earlier. Do you remember it?

♠K J 5
♡A 10 7
♢Q 7 4 2
♣K J 2

The right sort of hand for playing in no-trumps is an evenly distributed one, with high cards well shared out – this is often described as 4–3–3–3. What could be more ideal for suggesting no-trumps where fewer tricks are required for game than anywhere else?

Good, you agree that the hand is suitable for no-trumps

play. There is an important difference though, between opening the bidding with one of a suit and 1NT. One of a suit simply suggests your best suit and tells your partner that you have at least thirteen points. (Later on you will learn that there *are* other, more exciting opening bids at a higher level, but that would be like trying to run before you can walk.)

An opening bid of 1NT, by contrast, is a very precise bid. Quite why this is so will become (I hope) very clear when you read the start of the next chapter. What I recommend you to play is what is often called a "Weak No-Trump." Don't worry, it is not suggested that you open 1NT with a collection of seaweed. No, if you follow the ideas set out, an opening bid of 1NT shows the balanced hand that we have been discussing – high cards well shared out, and 13–15 points. Note that well, 13–15 points. Not less than 13 (for then you wouldn't have opened the bidding anyhow) and equally important, not *more* than 15.

There are other ideas about the strength of an opening bid of 1NT. A number of players prefer to play what they call the *strong* no trump rather than what I am suggesting – the weak no trump. For the time being, don't worry. If you and your partner stick to the arrangement that an opening bid of 1NT always shows a balanced hand with *between 13–15 points, no more and no less*, then you are off to an excellent start.

If you are on your own for the time being, away you go again. Deal hands, decide your opening bid and remember that 1NT is now included in your repertoire. (A *balanced* hand with 13–15 points, no more, no less.)

Go on, deal a few hands and make your decisions before you read on.

"BAD LUCK, PARTNER! YOUR PLAY WOULD HAVE BEEN RIGHT IF EITHER THERE WERE TWELVE CLUBS IN THIS PACK OR FOURTEEN. IT WAS DESPERATELY UNLUCKY TO FIND EXACTLY THIRTEEN IN THE SUIT."

# Chapter 5

## BUILDING UP TRICKS – "SUIT ESTABLISHMENT"

It is all very well to be able to make an opening bid but, just for the sake of argument, suppose that you open 1NT and everybody else says "No Bid". As we have seen, that is the end of the bidding, and now the play gets under way.

There are one or two new words that need to be introduced at this stage – but don't worry, they are easy to remember – and they apply to the *play* of the cards after the bidding has finished.

The *declarer* is the player who first mentioned the suit that finally became trumps. So if the bidding had gone:

| *SOUTH* | *WEST* | *NORTH* | *EAST* |
|---|---|---|---|
| 1NT | No Bid | No Bid | No Bid |

it would be very simple – South, the only player who had bid anything, would be declarer. But try:

| *SOUTH* | *WEST* | *NORTH* | *EAST* |
|---|---|---|---|
| 1♠ | 2♡ | 2♠ | No Bid |
| No Bid | No Bid | | |

Again South is the declarer – spades ended as trumps, South was the one who invented the idea of spades as trumps.

You see, it doesn't matter who *deals* the cards: when you decide who is to be declarer, everything depends on the *bids* that have been made.

Right, suppose that you are the declarer – what does this mean? It means that you will *play* the cards. And once you know who is to be the declarer, you know who is going to make the *opening lead*, i.e. play the first card to the first trick – it is the player on the left of the declarer.

Try out these quick tests after reading the auction, answering two questions. Who is declarer and who leads?

| | *SOUTH* | *WEST* | *NORTH* | *EAST* |
|---|---|---|---|---|
| (1) | | No Bid | No Bid | No Bid |
| | 1♡ | No Bid | 1♠ | No Bid |
| | 2♠ | No Bid | No Bid | No Bid |

| | *SOUTH* | *WEST* | *NORTH* | *EAST* |
|---|---|---|---|---|
| (2) | No Bid | No Bid | 1♡ | 2♣ |
| | 2♠ | 3♠ | 4♠ | No Bid |
| | No Bid | No Bid | | |

| | *SOUTH* | *WEST* | *NORTH* | *EAST* |
|---|---|---|---|---|
| (3) | 1◇ | 1♡ | 2♣ | 3♡ |
| | No Bid | No Bid | No Bid | |

I hope that you got these all right.

(1) North is declarer in Two Spades and East leads.

(2) South is declarer in Four Spades and West leads.

(3) West is declarer in Three Hearts and North leads.

Now comes the final piece of routine.

*After the opening lead has been made* (and this is the big difference from whist and similar card games), the declarer's partner puts his entire hand down, face upwards on the table. He becomes known as the *dummy* and has no further part in the play of the cards.

Have you got the sequence of events? Someone deals, they start the bidding (perhaps with a No Bid, it all depends on their hand), the bidding winds on until three players in succession have passed. Then you know who is to be declarer and who makes the opening lead. They lead, and dummy comes down.

Make a habit of spreading dummy's cards like this:

| ♠ | ♡ | ♢ | ♣ |
|---|---|---|---|
| A | K | A | 8 |
| K | 7 | Q | 5 |
| J | 4 | 6 | |
| 3 | | 2 | |

There is only one other thing that dummy should remember. If there is a trump suit he should put trumps down on *his right*. So, with the same hand, if hearts are trumps, he should put his hand down as:

| ♡ | ♠ | ♢ | ♣ |
|---|---|---|---|
| K | A | A | 8 |
| 7 | K | Q | 5 |
| 4 | J | 6 | |
| | 3 | 2 | |

(After the trumps, the order of the other suits doesn't

really matter; in a no-trump contract you can put them down in any order you like.)

Now, what has dummy got to do? And the answer is – nothing! The declarer is in sole charge of his hand *and* the dummy. Suppose that you are South and the bidding has left you as declarer. West leads a card, dummy exposes his goodies, and now it is up to you. Select a suitable card from dummy, (or "from the table" as it is sometimes known) watch East play a card, and now choose one from your own hand.

Dummy may be passive, but if it is a card from dummy that wins the first trick, then it must be a card from dummy that starts off the play to the second trick. Equally, if you arranged to win the first trick in your own hand, then you must start the play to the next trick from your own hand.

Just suppose that you have ended up in a contract of 1NT. You need to collect seven out of the thirteen tricks to make your contract but it will rarely happen that you can look at the dummy and say "Ah! Between us we have four Aces and three Kings – I can take the first seven tricks without breathing hard." Far more often you will find yourself inspecting perhaps four sure winners and only a series of hopes for the extra tricks that you need.

Right! Extra tricks. Just think of a suit where you hold K Q J 10 and dummy has (say) 4 3 2. There is nothing that you can take immediately, for one of the opponents holds the Ace. But if you can get to work on this suit at an early stage, it is not too difficult for you to *establish* three tricks. I am sure that you get the idea. You lead one of your high cards (and it really doesn't matter whether you choose the King, the Queen, the Jack or the Ten – they are all equal in value as far as you are concerned). Either the opponents (one of whom holds the Ace) let you hold this trick or they take it with their Ace. But once the Ace has gone you have *established* three tricks for your remaining high cards in the suit.

There are many examples like this. Try:

♠Q 10 9 4
♠J 7 3

You lead high cards and your opponents will have to play their Ace and their King – you will then be left with two winners. It is no use leading the three and playing dummy's four in the hope that the other side play their Ace or King. They won't! They will win the trick cheaply with something like the six or eight and still have the Ace and King to make later. The whole secret here is that your side owns four equivalent cards – the Queen, Jack, ten and nine – and the other side have only two cards that can beat any of them. Try a few more. How many tricks do you expect to make with the following?

♠J 8 6 2
♠10 9

It doesn't look promising, and yet there is enough material for a trick – if you work at it! Just think, the ten loses to the Queen; the nine loses to the King; the Jack loses to the Ace. . . . And what are you left with? The eight, which is a winner.

There are one or two traps. Suppose that you started with:

♠J 8 2
♠10 9 6

Is there enough material for a trick here? No, because your opponents can swiftly play off the Ace, King and Queen and all of your cards will have gone. Can you see the difference between this example and the one before? In the first case you were able to play your Jack, ten, nine and eight on separate tricks. In the second example, two of them had to go together.

Give a thought to a suit that looks like this:

♠Q 7 4
♠J 6 3

How many tricks are certain? Unfortunately you cannot be sure of anything. Your Jack may lose to the King, your Queen to the Ace, and what have you got left? Only rubbish, and no chance of a trick. Make a tiny change – give yourself the ten instead of the six.

♠Q 7 4
♠J 10 3

Can you see the difference? Three *equivalent* cards that can be played on separate tricks and your opponents have only two cards to beat them – eventually you must come to a trick.

It is not too difficult to see how the high cards work for you but perhaps not so easy to think of low cards proving useful.

Suppose that you are playing in no-trumps and that this is the suit at which you are looking:

♠A K Q
♠5 4 3

Quite right, there really is no problem at all. You have

three tricks and there will never be less and there will never be more. Now let's make a tiny change, adding a low card. Look at this:

♠A K Q 2
♠5 4 3

Still the same three top winners, but have you any chance of getting something extra? Time for a little arithmetic (nothing too taxing, only adding up to thirteen). Your side has seven cards in the suit – that means that your opponents hold only six cards. And what is the best thing that can happen if two opponents hold six cards between them? It is that they hold three each. It really doesn't matter which three cards West holds and which three cards East holds – for example:

|  | ♠A K Q 2 |  |
|---|---|---|
| ♠J 9 7 |  | ♠10 8 6 |
|  | ♠5 4 3 |  |

as long as they have got three each. You play off the Ace, King and Queen – no-one has any cards left in the suit and so your two is a winner.

There are a great many suits like this where little cards turn into tricks. Try the following examples:

♠A K 7 6 4
♠5 3 2

There are two obvious tricks to take with the Ace and the King, but what prospects are there of getting the low cards to work? Arithmetic time again – your side has eight cards in the suit, so the opponents have five. What you must hope is that their cards are divided 3–2.

Try it out – suppose that the set-up is like this:

♠A K 7 6 4

♠Q 10 9 ♠J 8

♠5 3 2

You take the Ace and the King, both opponents follow suit, and the Queen is still missing. But it is all by itself – all you need do is lead dummy's four, lose a trick to the Queen and the remaining cards (the seven and the six) are established as winners.

Can you see a possible snag? Good! It is no use having two winners if you can't get the lead into that hand to make them. We will have to come back to this sort of problem later, but just give a thought to a suit like this:

♢5 4 2
♢A 10 9 8 7 6 3

You are missing a lot of important cards – the King, the Queen and the Jack – but your opponents have no cards to protect them. As long as the three missing cards are shared out 2–1, then, when you play off your Ace, two honours fall. There will then only be one high card left out against you and any of your remaining cards force your opponents to play it. Now all the cards that you have left will be tricks.

However, there is one thing that you must keep in mind – in this example you made no fewer than five tricks with low cards but (and it is an important "but") you must let the other side make a trick first. It is really a good investment when you think about it.

Very briefly, let's go the other way and reduce the number of cards that our side holds in a suit. Consider:

♠A K Q 2
♠4 3

Three top winners, fine, but any chance of anything extra coming in from a low card? Hardly, for the other side holds seven cards to your six. No matter how evenly they are shared, playing off the Ace, King and Queen will leave one opponent with at least one card. And whatever it is, it will be higher than the two!

Summing up, if you and your partner have started with more cards in a suit than your opponents you have a *chance* of making something extra with your low cards. Only a chance, not a certainty, but the bigger the majority of cards that you hold, the better your chance.

You are much better placed now to try playing hands. Judge whether you have an opening bid, select the best trump suit (or no-trumps if you have the right sort and strength of hand) and see how many tricks you can build up and make.

"YOUR LEAD, PARTNER."
S.O.S.
CAT

# Chapter 6

## YOUR PARTNER OPENS THE BIDDING – WHAT DO YOU DO?

This chapter has to be divided into two distinct parts. There is a big difference between your partner opening 1NT (and showing 13–15 points with a balanced hand) and starting off the bidding with one of a suit when all you know is that he holds *at least* 13 points and has told you about his longest suit.

First things first. Suppose that partner (North) has opened 1NT. When do you want to reply? Two factors come into your answer – (i) whether you are happy with his suggestion of playing in no-trumps, and (ii) how good your hand is.

First, let us suppose that, like partner, you also have a balanced hand – no long suits, no short suits. You are very happy with the idea of playing in no-trumps, and there is no reason to suggest a suit.

Now is the time to introduce the second "magic number" of Bridge. You have met the first one, thirteen, the number of points that a player needs to *open* the bidding. Now the second, *26*, is easy to remember because it is just two lots of thirteen. Twenty-six is the number of points that a partnership need before it is sensible for them to have a shot at making game in one go. Note the use of the word "sensible." Every once in a while you and your partner will bid your way to a perfectly reasonable game with perhaps 28 points between you. But when you start playing the hand, everything seems to go wrong. All five missing trumps turn out to be bunched in one hand, all the missing high cards pop up in the wrong places. . . . Disaster after disaster, and you don't make enough tricks for game. Don't lose sleep over the problem – you *bid* perfectly sensibly and you would have made your contract *most* of the time. So today is Friday the thirteenth!

By contrast, every so often your partner will overbid like a lunatic. (This is the beauty of bridge – if anything goes wrong in a big way there is usually some way in which your partner is responsible. You, personally, are rarely at fault. Or so you like to think.) You end up in some wildly optimistic game contract with perhaps only twenty-three points between the two hands. It looks a disaster but as you play the hand, well against the odds, everything divides evenly and all the missing high cards are well placed for you. You make your unlikely game and tend to forget your partner's optimism.

Nevertheless, in spite of your good days and your bad days, twenty-six is about the "break-even" point. Put it like this. If you and your partner always bid to game when you hold at least 26 points and you manage to put on the brakes whenever you hold less then, *over the years*, things will go well for you. You won't get things right every time – nobody does! – but you will have the odds in your favour.

Time for some hands. Your partner opens 1NT (showing 13–15 points) and you hold:

♠A 7 4
♡K J 3
♢Q 10 8 6
♣K 8 2

Have you counted your points? Good, you have 13. Partner has 13–15, therefore you have at least 26 between you. You have a diamond suit (of sorts) but to make game in diamonds you need eleven tricks. Surely, as you are happy with the no-trump idea, nine tricks in no-trumps seems a better bet.

Simple arithmetic. Partner likes no-trumps and holds between 13 and 15 points, you like no-trumps and you hold 13 points. What could be easier? Over your partner's 1NT opening bid you respond 3NT. Straightforward stuff. You know that your partnership holds enough points, you know that you both like no-trumps.

Try again. Partner opens 1NT (13–15 points) and you hold:

♠Q 7 4 2
♡K J 5
◇Q 6 3
♣J 7 2

Good, you like no-trumps, but know that between you there are not enough points for game. Easy! You say No Bid. Leave partner peacefully alone in his contract of 1NT.

Is there a half-way house? Is it always a question of plunging on to game or leaving partner alone in 1NT? Well, there is this possibility – suppose that you had been dealt:

♠K J 4
♡Q 9 8 7
◇A 6 3
♣J 10 4

Partner opens 1NT (13–15 points) and you have to decide

whether you have the vital 26 between you. Now, you are looking at eleven points. As a partnership you will hold 24, 25 or 26 points. How can you test the market? I expect that you have guessed. You raise to 2NT. Not because you hope to make 2NT (you do!) but because you have hopes of making three. Your single raise urges partner to go on if he is maximum with a full fifteen points but warns him to pass if he has only thirteen.

Most of the time you can make an immediate decision – rushing to game or leaving partner peacefully alone in 1NT. It is only once in a while that it is necessary to take a second opinion.

The trouble is that we have only considered half the problem of responding to 1NT. Some of the time you will not be pleased at all with your partner's suggestion of playing in no-trumps. Suppose that you had been dealt:

♠ none
♡10 8 7 6 3 2
◇6 4 2
♣J 8 5 3

It is an awful hand with only one point in high cards. What do you think would happen if you left your partner to play in 1NT? To start with it is wildly unlikely that he will be able to use your long heart suit, and your Jack of clubs won't get him gushing with admiration. What is worse, the opponents must have a lot of spades – they will lead them and even if your partner has got a guard in the suit it will quickly be driven out.

Is there any escape from watching partner go three or four down in his 1NT contract? Yes, you will do much better if only you can play with hearts as trumps. True, you have got a bad suit, but it does contain six cards (probably three more than anyone else at the table) and if hearts are trumps your hand will certainly produce *some* tricks.

Of course you have to go to Two Hearts to get past 1NT – trying for eight tricks rather than seven, but would you rather go one off in Two Hearts or watch your partner go three or four off in 1NT?

Of course, you couldn't risk bidding Two Hearts if there were the slightest danger of your partner lurching on to Three Hearts or 2NT, or bidding some new suit of his own.

Fortunately there is a very simple arrangement, universally played, over an opening bid of 1NT. If you respond with *two* of any suit, you are requesting partner not to do any more bidding. On second thoughts, that is much too delicate a way of putting things. 1NT – 2 of a suit says "SHUT UP!! I don't want to hear another word – until we start the next hand."

Fine, you know how to put the brakes on if you don't like no-trumps. But where is the accelerator? I am sure that you can see the problem – you don't like no-trumps and yet you have a good hand – good enough to make game with the 13–15 points that you know are facing you.

Take this hand:

♠A J 9 6 3
♡A J 9 6 3
◇Q 5 2
♣ none

Twelve points, two five card suits, but a void in clubs. There should be a play for game somewhere but ten tricks with either spades or hearts as trumps will be more attractive than nine in no-trumps. With nothing to choose between your major suits you would like to tell partner about both of them to see which one he prefers. The trouble is that is you start off peacefully with a bid of Two Spades or Two Hearts, then that will be that. As we have seen, a well behaved partner will say No Bid without a second glance.

The solution? You *jump* the bidding in one of your suits. Here, just as though you were opening the bidding with two touching suits, you bid three spades. If you had only a four card suit you wouldn't have been worried about the idea of playing in no-trumps. It is only when you have five or more cards in your suit that you want to explore.

And there is another thought – it is not always worth while telling partner about one of the minor suits. Compare these two hands:

| (a) | ♠A 5 | (b) | ♠Q 10 8 6 5 |
|---|---|---|---|
| | ♡J 6 4 | | ♡J 6 4 |
| | ◇Q 10 8 6 5 | | ◇A 5 |
| | ♣A J 2 | | ♣A J 2 |

With hand (a) it is sensible to raise 1NT directly to 3NT. Eleven tricks with diamonds as trumps is a doubtful enterprise – nine tricks in no-trumps, a fair bet.

On to hand (b). Now ten tricks with spades as trumps (as long as partner likes the suit) may easily be better than nine in no-trumps.

Can you see the difference? A good trump suit between the two hands is going to be worth (on average) an extra trick. So trying for nine tricks in no-trumps is often a better bet than trying for eleven tricks with either diamonds or clubs as trumps. But with a fair fit in one of the major suits (spades or hearts) the ownership of a reasonable trump suit may make one trick difference. So, Four Spades or Four Hearts (with a sensible trump suit) might well lead to an easier game.

We are well placed now to put everything into summary form. Just think of your two decisions – it is all black and white stuff! – do you approve of partner's suggestion or not; do you want to be in a game contract or not?

Put it in the form of a table:

| | Not good enough for game | Good enough for game |
|---|---|---|
| Like No-Trumps | *No Bid* | *3NT* |
| Hate No-Trumps | *2 of a long suit* | *3 of a long suit* |

The beauty of hearing your partner open 1NT is that you are in complete charge! You know what he has got (the strength of his hand and that it is balanced) and you can see what you have got. What could be easier for you?

The other big advantage of an opening bid of 1NT is that it tends to keep the opposition quiet. If you open, say, One Club, it is very easy for the next player to join in with One Diamond or One Heart or . . . anything that he likes at the One level. But if you have opened 1NT, then he can only take action at the Two level. And there must be quite a few hands on which he would be prepared to compete with One of something but feels that it would be too risky to join in at the Two level.

I am not suggesting that it pays to open 1NT with the wrong sort of hand or the wrong number of points for, over the years, you will lose far more than you gain. Nevertheless, because of its partnership advantages, you should find yourself looking for excuses to open 1NT rather than find reasons not to. . . .

* * *

Of course, there is another big problem in responding. Your partner may decide to start off with One of a suit rather than 1NT. How do you reply? It is a big question!

First, let us think what partner's opening bid shows. No longer (as when he opened 1NT) do you know *exactly* what he has got. Instead, all you know is his longest suit (or one of them) and that he has got at least 13 points.

In practice there is an upper limit to what he might hold, for with more than 20 points he might have found something more exciting with which to open the bidding. (Two of a suit or 2NT – but more of those possibilities later.)

Right, for the sake of argument let us suppose that our partner has opened the bidding with One Heart, and the next player has said No Bid. How should we respond – what possibilities are available?

I would say that whatever action we take comes under four headings.

(1) No Bid
(2) Support partner
(3) Respond in no-trumps
(4) Bid a new suit

Let us take them one at a time. Suppose that you hold:

♠10 7 6 5 4 2
♡ none
◊J 8 6 3 2
♣5 4

Remember, partner has opened One Heart. One thing is certain, you don't fancy the idea of this hand being played with hearts as trumps. And yet you can't make bricks without straw – if you make a bid, surely your partner is going to think that you have something of interest in your hand (high cards, material with which to make tricks.)

You *know* that you have got remarkably little but bridge (like other walks of life) is fraught with temptation. Before you can stop yourself, you hear your voice saying "One Spade." Of course, it wouldn't be too bad if partner supported your spades but in real life he always seems to bid "Two Hearts". Now you get the feeling that, if he doesn't like your spades and you don't like his hearts, surely there must be a better spot somewhere. And you hear yourself trying "Three Diamonds." Now, be fair, if you hear your partner push on with 3NT or Three Hearts, will you be happy? I should think not, for you have made two constructive bids without any values in your hand. As things have gone, you are heading for a disaster on the grand scale! Solution? Pass One Heart! It may not be the ideal contract, but it will not be a total catastrophe.

To put things in terms of simple arithmetic, if your partner opens the bidding with One of a suit, you should pass unless you hold at least six points in high cards. His opening bid may contain as many as 20 points and (in case you have a game available – remember – 26 points) you keep things alive.

Consider the second on our list – the idea of supporting partner. Now we come on to another important question – how can you be sure that your partnership has found a sensible trump suit? A little more arithmetic, I'm afraid, but again, nothing very taxing. Just think of choosing one of the suits as trumps. If you and your partner hold only seven between you it will mean that your opponents hold six. And a majority of seven-six is not very healthy. You have only got to be made to trump once, perhaps twice, and suddenly you find your side with fewer trumps than the opposition. Your reason for choosing that suit as trumps has gone out of the window! However, if your partnership has started with at least *eight* out of the thirteen trumps you would be on much firmer ground. Consider – your side owns eight, your opponents only five. You may be made to trump once, or even twice but your side will still have the majority of the trumps.

How, then, can you be sure of having at least eight trumps between the two hands? Only by not supporting your partner immediately unless you have at least four cards in his suit. At least this is a jolly good idea that you should only give up in an emergency.

Let's look at a few hands where you are happy with partner's suggestion of a trump suit. Suppose he has opened One Spade and you hold:

♠Q 10 7 3
♡8 4
♢A J 5 3
♣10 9 4

Partner *may* have as many as 20 points and still not have opened with anything more exciting. Just in case he has, you keep the bidding open when you hold six or more points. You certainly like spades and you certainly haven't got a great hand. Content yourself with a raise to two spades. Most of the time your partner will pass, but when he is very strong he will push on to game. (Four Spades.) Your bid shows something between six and nine points.

Now improve your hand a little. Add another Ace, making it a whole trick stronger:

♠Q 10 7 3
♡A 4
◇A J 5 3
♣10 9 4

The change means that you are too good to bid just Two Spades. Instead you raise to Three Spades – a much more encouraging bid showing 10–12 points. Your partner will usually push onto game now, but not if he has started with a completely minimum 13 points and no great distribution.

Finally, make the hand even better:

♠Q 10 7 3
♡A 4
◇A J 5 3
♣K 9 4

That gives you 14 points and even if partner has nothing at all to spare for his opening, *you* know that between you there are at least the 26 points that you need for game. There is no need to hold back and you raise directly to Four Spades.

Summing up, if you like partner's spade suit:

**with 6–9 points, bid 2 ♠**
**with 10–12 points, bid 3 ♠**
**with 13–15 points, bid 4 ♠**

Before we leave the business of supporting partner's suit, just think of this problem. Suppose that you bid One Heart and hear partner support you, which of these two hands would you prefer to find as your dummy?

| (a) | | (b) | |
|---|---|---|---|
| | ♠A 6 5 | | ♠A 6 5 2 |
| | ♡K 10 6 3 | | ♡K 10 6 3 |
| | ◇Q 8 7 | | ◇Q 8 7 4 |
| | ♣4 3 2 | | ♣2 |

Both have exactly nine points and would seem to fit in very nicely with a raise to Two Hearts. But if this is your hand

♠K Q 4
♡A Q J 5 4
◇K 2
♣10 8 6

it is a good exercise to try to work out how many tricks you will make in each case. Facing hand (1), your opponents will be in a position to take the first four tricks (three clubs and a diamond) before you start. And it doesn't matter how many high cards you have left, you can't make ten tricks if the other side have already taken four.

By contrast, suppose hand (b) is your dummy. Can you see the vital difference? No longer can the other side take three club tricks. They can only take one, for any more clubs that they lead will be trumped in dummy. Indeed, you make two *extra* tricks from your trumps – the five in your hand and two

EPBB-E

ruffs on the table.

The thing that made hand (b) so much better was the *singleton* club and the fact that there were plenty of trumps. It would have been much better if hand (b) had a *void* in clubs and not quite so good, but still useful, if it had a *doubleton* club.

We have already learnt one way of adjusting our point count. (When you open the bidding you add on something for a long suit.)

Now another way – *only to be used when supporting partner's suit.*

Count as follows: **for a void, add on 3 points**
**for a singleton, add on 2 points**
**for a doubleton, add on 1 point**

Time to reassess hand (b). Nine points in high cards, plus two points for the singleton, and so with eleven points in support of a heart contract, Three Hearts should be the bid. WARNING!!! Don't start adding on points for long suits *and* short suits on the same hand – you will come up with some silly answers. After all, if you have long suits, you will have short suits somewhere else in the hand and you will be counting the same thing twice.

Take this hand:

♠4
♡K Q 8 7 3
♢K Q 6 4 2
♣8 5

If you were thinking of opening, how many points? Right, twelve – so you pass. But suppose that your partner opens One Heart, how many points is your hand worth in support of hearts? Good, thirteen. And so you raise directly to Four Hearts.

Next on the list of possible things to do when you heard partner open One of a suit was for you to respond in no-trumps.

Responses in no-trumps, just like opening bids in no-trumps, are always based on balanced hands, no long suits, no short suits, with the high cards reasonably well shared out.

You'll start to see a familiar pattern as we look at some examples. Suppose partner opens One Spade and you have one of the following hands:

| (a) | (b) | (c) |
|---|---|---|
| ♠8 7 3 | ♠K 8 7 | ♠K 8 7 |
| ♡K J 4 | ♡K J 4 | ♡K J 4 |
| ♢Q J 7 | ♢Q J 7 | ♢A Q 7 |
| ♣J 9 4 2 | ♣J 9 4 2 | ♣J 9 4 2 |

I expect that you can work out your responses:
with (a) respond 1NT – showing 6–9 points
with (b) respond 2NT – showing 10–12 points
with (c) respond 3NT – showing 13–15 points
Just like supporting partner's suit.

All these six bids are called *Limit Bids* for they tell partner exactly what you have got. And when you have made a limit bid, you can sit back and relax. Partner is in charge! He knows what you have got, and he certainly knows what he has got.

# Chapter 7

## YOUR PARTNER OPENS AND YOU WANT TO BID A NEW SUIT

You may have wondered what happened to the fourth possibility on our list of possible responses to one of a suit from partner – that of replying in a new suit.

When you supported partner's suit or responded in no-trumps you did so to the full extent of your hand – indeed, we called them *limit* bids. The trouble is that you can't use the same idea when you bid a *new* suit. For example, partner opens One Spade and you want to tell him about a club suit. Do you bid Two Clubs with 6–9 points, Three Clubs with 10–12 points and Four Clubs with 13–15 points?

Hardly, for the start of One Spade – Four Clubs takes you to the Four level and you still haven't sorted out a suit that both of the partnership like. Quite possibly, 3NT might be the best game contract, but you have gone galloping right past that. So, when you reply in a *new* suit there is no rush. With:

| (a) | (b) | (c) |
|---|---|---|
| ♠A Q 7 6 4 | ♠A Q 7 6 4 | ♠A Q 7 6 4 |
| ♡3 | ♡3 | ♡3 |
| ◇8 7 6 5 | ◇A 7 6 5 | ◇A 7 6 5 |
| ♣9 5 3 | ♣9 5 3 | ♣A 5 3 |

you make exactly the same simple response of One Spade in reply to One Heart.

Can you see what follows from this? Suppose that you have opened the bidding with a suit, and that your partner replies in a new suit. *You cannot pass*. At least, not if you want to stay on speaking terms with your partner for, no matter how bad an opening bid you have got, he *may* have enough points for you to make a game. Think of it as the start of an intelligent conversation. You don't telephone a friend and, as soon as he replies, hang up!

Time to look at a hand. Suppose that you hold:

♠A 8 6 4
♡Q 9 6 2
♢7 3
♣Q 10 5

and partner opens One Diamond. What possible replies can you make? You could bid One Spade, you could bid One Heart, or you could bid 1NT. Which one is best? On the face of it, 1NT seems best for it is a limit bid and tells partner that you have 6–9 points. The alternative of bidding one of your suits is much vaguer, just showing at least six points. Nevertheless, it is better to bid a suit first, if you can do so conveniently, rather than rush into no-trumps straight away. Just picture partner with:

♠J 2
♡J 10 8 3
♢A K 9 8 5
♣A 3

It is not an exciting opening bid, but he will certainly start with One Diamond. Now, looking at both hands, what is the best trump suit? Good, hearts, for you have eight cards in the suit between the two hands and fewer cards in all the other suits. But can you be sure of finding the fit in hearts if you respond either 1NT or One Spade? You are making it very difficult for partner to mention the suit (it would have to be One Diamond – One Spade, *Two* Hearts, or One Diamond –1NT, *Two* Hearts.) But if you had started by responding One Heart, life would have been easy for partner. He could support hearts with four or more cards in the suit, he could show a spade suit at the One level or he could bid 1NT himself. The best of all worlds . . .

There are really two important points to be learnt from this example. (1) If you can show a suit conveniently at the One level then do so, rather than rush into no-trumps. (2) If you have a choice of two or more suits of the same length that you can show at the One level, make the cheapest bid. Try out the idea on this hand:

♠A 8 5 4
♡K 9 7 3
♢Q 8 5 2
♣5

Partner opens One Club. Your reply? Right. One Diamond. Partner can support your suit if he has four of them and it is easy for him to bid either hearts or spades at the One level if he wants to.

Next, let's think about a slightly different problem. If your partner opens One Heart, you can tell him about a spade suit by bidding One Spade. Of course it is a new suit, forcing partner to bid again, but all that you are promising is at least six points and at least four cards in your suit. It is often referred to as a 'One over One' response. But suppose you had wanted to tell partner about a diamond suit? Over One Heart you have to call *Two* Diamonds. Again, partner has to go on bidding but as it is you who has committed your side to eight tricks instead of just seven with your 'Two over One' response, it is only reasonable that you should have a slightly stronger hand than you needed for a response on the One level. A fair guide is for you not to splash out at the Two level unless you have at least eight points in high cards and a five card suit.

You can bend either of these requirements a little if you have something to spare in the other. So with:

| (a) | | or | (b) | |
|---|---|---|---|---|
| | ♠7 4 | | | ♠8 3 |
| | ♡8 3 | | | ♡A 10 5 |
| | ◊8 2 | | | ◊K Q 8 7 |
| | ♣A Q J 10 9 8 7 | | | ♣A J 9 3 |

it would be perfectly all right to respond Two Clubs to One Heart. With (a) you have only seven points but a good long suit to compensate. With (b) you have plenty of points to spare and will be doing some more bidding, even though you only have a four card suit.

Can you see a possible problem coming along? Try responding to One Heart with this hand:

♠4
♡A J 3
◊J 7 5 2
♣10 8 5 4 3

"I DOUBLE FOUR SPADES!"

Worth a bid, with six points, but not worth a new suit at the Two level! So you can't bid Two Clubs and you are too good to pass. About the only way out of your difficulty is to break (or rather bend) one of your earlier rules and support partner with only three trumps by raising to Two Hearts. Don't pretend that it is a good bid – it isn't – but the alternatives (of Two Clubs and No Bid) are worse.

Think of the same hand, but this time partner opens One Spade. You are still not worth a new suit at the Two level and now there is no question of supporting partner's suit. Solution? You 'bend' your 1NT response a little. You have the right number of points (remember, 6–9 points) but the wrong distribution. Unlucky, but what can you do? Certainly if partner passes 1NT or bids another suit you will have improved on One Spade. You will only feel depressed if partner pushes on and bids his spades again. Mind you, if your hand had been even a little stronger, say:

♠4
♡A J 3
◇J 7 5 2
♣K 8 5 4 3

you wouldn't have a care in the world. Over One Heart or One Spade you have all the values that you need for a new suit at the Two level.

It would be a good idea now to take a hand and follow it through several rounds of bidding, refreshing your memory as to which bids are limit bids and which are not. Right, you are dealt this collection:

♠A J 8 3
♡Q J 8 5 2
◇7
♣A Q 7

and hear partner open One Diamond. The first move is easy enough – you bid One Heart. It is a new suit so there is no rush. But now partner follows up by raising to Two Hearts – what now?

To help you think about this problem clearly, cast your mind back to something we said much earlier – that when you are bidding, you and your partner are trying to answer two questions.

(1) In which suit do we want to play?
(2) How high do we want to get?

Believe me, if you get the answers to these two right nine times out of ten, there is a place waiting for you on the British team! How many answers are there to (1) and (2)? There are four suits but there is also the possibility of playing in no-trumps so there are five possible solutions. However, the problem of how high is a little more complicated. You could say that there are seven levels – One, Two, up to Seven – but broadly speaking there are only two targets. Either you want to bid a game, or you want to stop short of game. And there is little or no point in bidding to, say, Four Diamonds instead of Three Diamonds – there is only the incentive to bid up if you think that you can make Five Diamonds for a game.

That is not quite the full story, of course, for one or two other things might happen. If you feel that your side can make twelve tricks (a small slam) or even thirteen tricks (a

"PERHAPS I
SHOULD DOUBLE."

grand slam) then there are substantial extra bonuses to be earned. Another possibility is that your opponents join in the bidding and you will have a competitive situation to judge. Indeed, there are two new bids that we have not mentioned yet! If your opponents bid something that you don't think they are going to make you can say 'Double'. Then if, (as you hope) they fail to make their contract you will score far more points than if you hadn't doubled. Furthermore, if the other side have the nerve to double you, there is the possibility of saying 'Redouble' which doubles the points at stake yet again. You don't have to redouble – you only do it when you are supremely confident about your bidding and values! That is where it all ends – you don't have re-redoubles however much you would like to!

Come back to our hand now with the two questions (1) and (2) clearly in mind. When your partner opens One Diamond you know that he has at least thirteen points. As you have fourteen you know that your side has the values for game and you can answer (2). No progress on (1) so far for you don't like partner's suggestion of diamonds and so you tell him about your hearts. To your delight he supports you, and (1) is answered as well. Which suit? Hearts. How high? Game. And so your next bid is Four Hearts.

Change the problem slightly – same hand, same opening bid, same response of One Heart. But now partner doesn't support your hearts and rebids One Spade instead. You like spades (with four of them) and you knew all along that you wanted to be in a game. Solution? Bid Four Spades.

Let us give the hand just one more twist – this time, over your One Heart, partner rebids Two Clubs. What now? You can't support clubs for you have only three, and you don't like partner's diamonds; he doesn't seem to like your hearts and he has had a chance (which he rejected) of bidding One Spade. And yet you still want to end up in a game. There are two possible answers – you could bid 3NT for you certainly have all four suits well held between you and you have the 13–15 points that your bid shows, or you could bid Two Spades. Do you see the difference between these bids? When you bid no-trumps or support partner, whether it is on the first or second round, you must bid to the *limit* of your hand. But when you bid a new suit you are keeping the pot boiling and there is no need to jump, for partner will not pass.

By the way, I am sure you are all wondering how you respond if you hold sixteen or more points, for all the limit bids seem to end at fifteen points. This is the one exception to not jumping in a new suit. With:

♠K 3
♡A K J 8 5
◇A Q 7
♣J 8 2

you would bid *Two* Hearts over One Club, or *Three* Hearts over One Spade – in each case one more than necessary. This commits your partnership to game – there is no way that either of you can put the brakes on now!

# Chapter 8

## MORE ABOUT WINNING TRICKS

So far we have thought about two distinct ways of making tricks with cards that are not obvious winners. For example, to refresh your memory, there was a suit of:

K Q J
4 3 2

There was nothing that you could take immediately for one of the opponents held the Ace but it wasn't difficult to *establish* two tricks. You simply led the suit from either hand and after the other side had won with their Ace you had two winners that you could take when you liked.

Next we considered the idea of making tricks with low cards – it only worked when your side held more cards in a suit than the opponents and even then it wasn't a certainty. We had looked at simple cases like this:

A K Q 2
5 4 3

I am sure you remember how it worked? Your side held seven cards in the suit, your opponents only six, and on your lucky days the missing six divided 3–3. Then, and only then, you came to an extra trick with the two.

Now a new idea. Think of the problem of playing a suit of:

A Q
3 2

There is one obvious winner – the Ace – but how do you go about organizing a second trick with the Queen? You have no idea whether it is East or West who holds the missing King. Try first by leading the Ace from the North hand. Any good? Hardly, for whichever opponent it is who holds the King is not likely to be kind enough to throw it under the Ace. Equally, leading the Queen first cannot help. Whoever it is that holds the King will simply play it now and again you end up with just the one trick.

If leading from the North hand doesn't help, what about leading a low card from South? The idea is that if West follows suit with anything other than the King you try the Queen from North. This is called taking a *finesse* and is something that whist players have been trying for hundreds of years – it is not a new idea for bridge only. Sometimes it works and produces an extra trick, sometimes it doesn't. Everything depends on who holds the missing King!

Try it out, first with the King where you want it (West) then with East when there is nothing that you can do about the problem:

(a)

| | | |
|---|---|---|
| | A Q | |
| K 6 | | 5 4 |
| | 3 2 | |

(b)

| | | |
|---|---|---|
| | A Q | |
| 5 4 | | K 6 |
| | 3 2 | |

There is another word that bridge has inherited from whist players – a *tenace*. It describes a combination of cards such as A Q. I like the "Irish" definition of a tenace; a sequence of three touching cards with the middle one taken away!

When you have got a tenace in one hand you can take a finesse by leading a low card towards it and, if the next hand plays low, trying the lower card from the tenace. Sometimes it works, sometimes it doesn't – it is a 50% chance of an extra trick.

Try one or two more. Suppose that you find yourself tackling a suit of:

4 3 2
A K J

How many tricks do you hope to make? Two certain ones with the Ace and King, fine, but have you any chance of a third trick? If you just play off the Ace and King it is most unlikely that the Queen will fall;but instead try out this new idea of the finesse. Here you have to get the lead into the North hand in order to play towards the tenace in the South hand. If East pops up with the Queen your problems are over. Far more likely, whether he holds the Queen or not, he will play low. This gives you the chance of finessing the Jack. It is the old story – 50% of the time it works, 50% of the time it fails. But it costs nothing to try, for on your good days you will end up with an *extra* trick.

Now think of:

A Q J
4 3 2

There are always two certain tricks for after your Queen has lost to the King the Jack will be a sure second winner. Nevertheless, you might do better. Get the lead into the South hand with another suit, lead low and finesse the Jack. It may lose to the King but you are no worse off – you still have the two tricks with which you started. But look on the bright side – your finesse may win! Giving you advance warning that it is a bit of a trick question, what do you lead next? Remember that the lead is in the North hand. The Ace? No, West won't throw his King away. The Queen? No, that doesn't help either for the defenders will simply take their King. The solution is to get the lead into the South hand with another suit and then try the finesse again. If, as you hope, West has got the missing King and East is not playing a deep game you will now make three tricks in the suit. It is what is called a *repeated finesse* – trying the same thing out twice in the same suit. It is not too difficult to find yourself doing the same thing three times – just think of:

A Q J 10
4 3 2

You have got the idea by now. Get the lead into the South hand, lead low and finesse the ten; get the lead back into the South hand with another suit, lead low and finesse the Jack. If everything is going according to plan, come back to the South hand before you lead the suit for a third time and finesse the Queen. Four tricks! As long as West held the missing King and it had been convenient to get the lead into the South hand three times.

There is a moral here. If you are sitting West and are unlucky enough to hold the King (rather than your partner) there is no point at all in playing it before you have to. Firstly, declarer may not have read this chapter on finessing and doesn't know how to take advantage of the well-placed King, secondly (even if he does know all about taking finesses), he simply may not be able to get the lead into the South hand enough times to pick up your King.

Next, think of this slightly more complicated example:

A Q 10
4 3 2

Here there is only one certain trick for your side for the Queen may lose to the King and the ten to the Jack. To give yourself the best possible chances, lead towards the A Q 10 and (if nothing pops up) try the ten. Whatever happens to this, when you next get the lead into the South hand, lead low and finesse the Queen. There are two important cards missing – the King and the Jack – but you have no idea how they are shared between East and West. There are four possibilities:

| | West | East |
|---|---|---|
| (1) | K J x | x x x |
| (2) | K x x | J x x |
| (3) | J x x | K x x |
| (4) | x x x | K J x |

If you try the suggested play you will find that with (1) you make three tricks, with (2) and (3) you make two tricks but with (4) – reserved for Friday the thirteenth – you make only one trick. You can cheer yourself up with the thought that if the cards lie with (4) you couldn't have done better no matter how you had played the suit but you won't cheer yourself up much!

A very similar suit is:

A J 10
4 3 2

Now that you have got the idea it shouldn't take you too long to work out the best play. Lead low from the South hand and try the ten (or the Jack) from North. Very likely it will lose – in fact three times out of four – but next time you get the lead into the South hand you finesse again. If you think it out you can judge your overall chances. Only when East holds both the King and the Queen will you fail to make two tricks. It is worth nothing that you can never make *three* tricks in the suit for, after all, your opponents hold both the King and the Queen and are bound to come to at least one trick.

Perhaps the simplest possible "finesse" position of them all is when you look at:

K 2
4 3

One thing is certain: if you lead a low card from the North hand no East player is going to be kind enough to rush in with the Ace. He will simply win the trick with some middle card and whoever holds the Ace will save it until the King is played. And leading the King certainly won't help.

It is the old story. Get the lead into the South hand and lead a low card towards the King. Will you make a trick? No, not always but whenever West holds the missing Ace you will, either on this round of the suit or later.

It is very much the same if you find yourself playing a suit of:

K Q 4
5 3 2

Brute force will give you one trick. You could lead the King, lose to the Ace and later make a trick with the Queen. Good, but you have a chance of doing better. Get the lead into the South hand and lead a low card towards the honours in the North hand. Half the time it will be West who holds the missing Ace. What can he do? Go in with the Ace? That is good news for you for you will now come to two easy tricks with the King and the Queen. If instead West plays low you have a bit more work to do. After North's King or Queen has won you have to get the lead back to the South hand in order to repeat the performance. Again, if West has the Ace he is struggling. If he goes in with the Ace North's other high card will win later while if he plays low it will win now.

Can you see the secret of suits like this? It can be summed up quite neatly. If you have nothing very much in one hand and some high cards in the other then you do better to lead from "nothing" towards "something". In this way you get one of the opponents to commit himself to playing a card before you have to choose what to play from the "something". You have met the idea much earlier in this chapter. Remember what we started with? The basic finesse position of Ace and Queen facing not very much. Your only chance of two tricks was to lead from nothing towards something.

Of course it is a principle that you can take too far. I can always remember a pupil looking at a suit of:

A K Q J
5 4 3 2

It was a no-trump contract and he carefully got the lead into his own hand (South) before touching the suit. It wasn't a great surprise when the Jack won, but the student resolutely came back to his hand before he led the suit again. It was about now that I managed to stop him. He was very indignant. "But that is just what you have been telling us!" he complained. "Lead from nothing towards something".

I think that he had missed the point. If the "something" is as good as A K Q J it really doesn't need looking after in any way – it can take care of itself and you can just lead it from the top without any possible risk. It is only when there is an important card or two missing from the "something" that it has to be looked after and led towards.

There is another suit combination that is worth considering:

A 3 2
Q J 10

The first thing that strikes you is that there is no tenace position. But it is still possible to take a finesse. You certainly have two tricks for you can really only lose one (to the King), but it is possible for you to make three tricks if the missing King is well placed for you. From what you have learnt so far about finessing it shouldn't be too difficult to get the idea. Arrange for the lead to be in the South hand before you tackle the suit, lead the Queen and let it run round (unless West plays the King on it when your problems will be solved). Whenever West has started with the King you will make three tricks but when the King is wrong (in other words with East), you will have to be content with two.

It is interesting to think of a similar suit:

A 3 2
Q 5 4

You have one certain trick with the Ace, you hope to make a second one with the Queen but you can hardly do better. How should you go about it then? The last idea of leading the Queen won't work for if East has the King he will win the trick, just leaving you with the Ace, and if West has the King he will play it on top of your Queen. Yes, his King is sacrificed but if you have had to use up both the Ace and the Queen to win one trick you haven't got much left! It is much more of a from nothing towards something situation. Forget about the Ace – that is always a trick. Take it if you like and then think about your Queen. The only way that it will come to life is if you lead *towards* it. If you play the suit that way you will make two tricks every time the King is right for you (that is with East) and only one when it is wrong. It is the old 50% chance that goes with every finesse that you take.

There is one final suit that it is worthwhile thinking about. Suppose that you find yourself looking at:

A J 2
K 10 3

Two easy tricks with the Ace and King, but can you do better? Yes, if you can guess who holds the missing Queen. If you think it is with West, you get the lead into the South hand and finesse the Jack; if you think it is with East, you lead low from North and finesse the ten. So you *can* always make three tricks if you are a good guesser. Or is it all guesswork? Just think – suppose one opponent has made two bids on his own while his partner has remained gloomily silent. Who would you say is the more likely to hold the missing Queen? Sometimes you can be even more certain. Perhaps East opens 1NT (showing 13–15 points). In spite of that you become declarer as South and a look at dummy shows you that your side has 26 points between you. There are 40 points in the pack, so who has the vital missing Queen? Good, I thought that you would get there. . . .

"MY TRICK!
YOU'VE GONE OFF!
HA! HA!

# Chapter 9

## CHOOSING A REBID

Making a *rebid* is another important idea that you have got to think carefully about. Clearly it is a good idea to know exactly what is meant by a rebid, and we are thinking about this situation – a player opens the bidding with One of a suit, his partner replies with a call in another suit and now the opening bidder is *expected to bid again*. This makes sense, for the opener (who has at least 13 points) has no idea how strong his partner may be. Certainly he will have at least six points (otherwise he wouldn't have replied at all) but he might have quite a few more and no matter how feeble the opening bid it is possible that the partnership have the 26 points that they need for game.

As No Bid is not acceptable, the things that you can do for a rebid come under four headings:

(1) Support partner's suit
(2) Rebid in no-trumps
(3) Rebid your own suit
(4) Bid a new suit

If you think about it, there really aren't any other possibilities. However, for all of (1) – (4), you can take action at different levels. We will take it stage by stage.

Let us take supporting partner's suit. Here is a familiar theme. As partner's bid has not promised more than four cards in his suit, you don't like supporting him unless you have four (or more) cards in the suit with him. Every once in a while you feel that you have to depart from this principle but only with reluctance and in emergencies. Good, with that idea clearly in mind, let us look at a few hands. Suppose that you started with:

♠8 2
♡K J 7 2
♢K 4
♣A Q 6 4 3

Quite right, you open One Club (your longest suit) and you are pleased to hear partner respond One Heart – a suit that you like with four cards. It is sensible to support his hearts but at the same time you want to get over the idea that you have only a minimum opening bid with thirteen or so points in high cards. So a single raise in hearts is quite enough – don't get carried away by your liking for hearts! So your rebid is Two Hearts and this suggests that your opening bid was in the 13–15 points department.

This is not a bad way to think about opening bids of One of a suit – weak, 13–15 points counting distribution; middle-sized, 16–18 points; and strong with 19–20 points. If you have started with more than 20 points you might well have found a more exciting bid than just One of your long suit but that is a treat in store for you!

Suppose that your opening bid had been a little better – perhaps:

♠A 2
♡K J 7 2
♢K 4
♣A Q 6 4 3

In fact you are a whole trick better – an extra Ace. You still just open One Club but, when you hear a One Heart reply, your rebid is Three Hearts. It sounds very encouraging, doesn't it, One Club – One Heart; Three Hearts? But it doesn't *force* your partner to bid again. All you are saying is that although clubs are your first bid suit you like his hearts (holding at least four cards in the suit) and that your opening bid was in the middle-sized range with 16–18 points. If partner has scraped up his One Heart response on a rather bare looking six points, he is quite free to refuse your invitation and pass. If, however, he has a little to spare he will be delighted to push on and bid Four Hearts to give you game.

Let us step up the hand still more and give you:

♠A 2
♡K J 7 2
♢A J
♣A Q 6 4 3

Now you are looking at nineteen points with a five card suit. You still only open One Club but as soon as you hear a squeak from partner – any squeak! – you want to be in game for you know that he has at least six points. Here your choice is easy. He likes hearts, you like hearts and between you there are enough points to make a game worth bidding. Simple stuff – Four Hearts is your rebid, suggesting that your opening bid contained something that was in the 19–20 points department.

Now let us try a switch. Suppose that you are not all that enthusiastic about your partner's suit but you have a reasonably balanced hand. For example:

♠A J 8
♡8 2
♢A K 9 3
♣Q 10 8 4

You might well have been reluctant to *open* 1NT with nothing very much in hearts and only two cards in the suit but after you have started with One Diamond and heard One Heart from partner it seems much more realistic to rebid 1NT (keeping the bidding at the One level) rather than splash out into Two Clubs and raise the level of the bidding on what, after all, is a dull and ordinary opening bid. The hand fits neatly into our minimum opening bid category of 13–15 points.

Now we play the same game that we did a page or so back. We improve our hand by adding an extra three points. Perhaps:

♠A J 8
♡K 2
♢A K 9 3
♣Q 10 8 4

You open One Diamond, partner responds One Heart and your rebid is 2NT – a balanced hand, suitable for no-trumps with somewhere between 16 and 18 points. Just as when you jumped the bidding in support of partner's suit this is not forcing. If partner has scraped up his One Heart response on a bare minimum of six points and is reasonably happy with your suggestion of playing in no-trumps he is quite free to pass. After all you are simply telling partner what you have got and, once he knows that, he judges whether we have got the magic 26 points that we need between us to make bidding a game a good bet.

Step things up again: suppose that you held:

♠A J 8
♡K 2
♢A K 9 3
♣A 10 8 4

You must be getting the idea now. You open One Diamond and, if you hear a reply from partner, rebid 3NT. The message – I have a balanced hand with 19–20 points. In exactly the same way as when you supported your partner's suit, the better the hand you have got, the more you bid. All of the six rebids we have looked at so far are limit bids (an idea we have met before) – telling partner how good and inviting him to go on towards game but only if he can judge that between you there are twenty-six points. A familiar tale – he knows what you have got, and should certainly be able to see what he has got!

On now to the third possibility on our list – rebidding your own suit. Straight away it is important to get the idea that rebidding your own suit as cheaply as possible is quite the most depressing thing that you can do. For example One Heart – One Spade; Two Hearts says quite clearly that you can't support partner, you can't rebid in no-trumps and that you have no other suit that you can show conveniently. Everybody likes to open the bidding with:

♠8 4
♡K J 10 8 6 2
◇A 6
♣K 6 4

(eleven points only but a six-card suit to improve matters). However you can't afford to open hands like this unless you have some way of putting the brakes on. To rebid Two Hearts suggests a hand just like this – about the only new bit of information that it gives partner is that you have at least five cards in your suit. When you bid it originally you promised four, when you bid it again you guarantee extra length. The rebid at the minimum level shows that your opening bid was in the 13–15 points range allowing for length.

It won't come as a surprise to learn that you can jump the bidding in your own suit but here you have to be careful. Just think – after the bidding One Heart, One Spade, how many hearts has the responder promised? Read the question carefully! Quite right, he wasn't promised any hearts at all.So, before you think about jumping the bidding in your suit, you have to have a very good suit. The sort of suit that you don't mind using as trumps even if your partner has only one or, even worse, a void. Think of this hand:

♠8 4
♡A K Q 10 7 3
◇A 5
♣K 6 4

With this you open One Heart, perhaps hear a reply of One Spade and rebid Three Hearts. The message is that you have a good six card suit and that you are in the 16–18 point range

– the middle-sized hand. It is not difficult to visualize the sort of hand on which you open One Heart and rebid Four Hearts after a response – perhaps an extra point or two, perhaps an extra card in your long suit, perhaps you have got one or two useful-looking high cards in the suit that partner has chosen for his response. In other words, just that little bit extra that puts your hand into the 19–20 (strong) range.

The only trouble now is that you might think that you have got the full picture – in other words, when you do the fourth thing on our original list and bid a new suit, you tell partner exactly how good your hand is at the same time. Unfortunately it doesn't quite work out like that. Think of our familiar start where you open One Heart and hear a One Spade response. You want to tell everyone about your other suit (perhaps clubs) and you have 19 points. Can you see the snag? If you rebid Four Clubs then the partnership is already committed to making ten tricks and you still haven't found a suit that you both like. What is worse, if there is no suit that you both like, the best final contract might have been 3NT (only nine tricks for the game) and you have gone wandering past that already. It is one thing to jump the bidding to a high level when you know what is going to be a good trump suit, but things have to change when you bid a new suit. It is very similar to responding in a new suit after your partner has opened. Don't panic! Don't panic! So with:

| (1) | (2) | (3) |
|---|---|---|
| ♠8 4 | ♠8 4 | ♠Q 4 |
| ♡A K 10 7 3 | ♡A K 10 7 3 | ♡A K 10 7 3 |
| ♢K Q 8 3 | ♢K Q 8 3 | ♢K Q 8 3 |
| ♣J 2 | ♣A 2 | ♣A 2 |

it is all just the same. You open One Heart and, when your partner responds One Spade, you peacefully rebid Two Diamonds. Partner will only pass if he prefers your diamonds to your hearts and has a very feeble hand indeed. It is worth keeping in mind, as responder, that even if you have a very poor hand you should always put partner back to his *first* suit when you have the same number of cards in both his suits. Take these two responding hands:

| (a) | | (b) | |
|---|---|---|---|
| | ♠A J 6 5 3 | | ♠A J 6 5 3 |
| | ♡2 | | ♡8 3 2 |
| | ◇J 9 5 4 | | ◇J 9 5 |
| | ♣8 7 6 | | ♣8 7 |

With (a) you pass Two Diamonds and hope for the best but with (b) you shouldn't leave partner there – instead you should put him back to Two Hearts. He might have more hearts than diamonds but he won't have more diamonds than hearts – he did *open* One Heart.

The very last possibility when you make a rebid is to *jump* the bidding in a new suit. This is the most dynamic rebid of them all. The message is that you have 19–20 points, enough for game even if partner has been hard pushed to scrape up a reply, but that it is not immediately obvious which game contract you want to try. You are not yet convinced that playing in partner's suit is a good idea (you haven't got four card support), your hand is not suitable for no-trumps and your own suit won't stand up on its own.

This is the sort of problem:

♠A J 4
♡A K 8 7 6
◇A K 4 3
♣3

You are not quite good enough for anything more exciting than an opening bid of One Heart. As soon as you hear any sort of reply, perhaps One Spade, nothing should hold you back for game must be bid. The trouble is that you are not at all sure just which game it should be. It would be silly to plunge into Four Spades and find that partner has only a poor four card suit. You can't rebid 3NT for you haven't got a balanced hand and, what is worse, the club suit may be wide open to attack. Finally, jumping to a game contract of Four Hearts may prove rather silly if partner turns up with only a singleton or void in hearts.

The solution to your problems, as you may have guessed, lies in jumping the bidding in a new suit. As you can see from this example, your other suit here is diamonds and the bidding will start One Heart – One Spade; Three Diamonds (only Two Diamonds was necessary to make a sufficient bid). The idea that you are getting over to partner is that you have the values to bid a game, you don't yet know what game it should be and that you want to hear something more from him. There are a number of things that he can do but he *can't* pass. He might support diamonds when Five Diamonds may prove to be the best game; he might bid 3NT if he has the clubs well held; he might rebid his spades – which would show that he held at least five cards in the suit – when you can go on to Four Spades with a clear conscience. Finally, he might bid Three Hearts. If he does so, how many hearts would you expect him to hold? Three only! For if he had started with four or more cards in your first suit he wouldn't have confused things by bidding spades after you had opened One Heart. After all, you can only make one suit trumps and when you have found one – one of the high-scoring major suits – that you both like, you cannot do any better.

# Chapter 10

## TRUMPS, AND HOW TO USE THEM

Trumps are funny things. They are obviously very powerful cards but sometimes they produce *extra* tricks, sometimes they don't.

Start off by thinking of a spade suit that looks like this:

♠4 3 2

♠A K Q J 10 9

How many tricks do you expect to make from the suit? Easy, isn't it? You have six winners, no more, no less.

Now turn it into a trump suit and suppose that there is a heart suit as well. Say:

♠4 3 2
♡4 3 2

♠A K Q J 10 9
♡2

The opponents lead hearts and, if you don't want to lose the second trick, you trump. But how many tricks does that make? One in the bag but you have only five winners left. And yet it seems awfully exciting – the pleasure of putting a low trump on an Ace or a King belonging to the other side. So much so that many beginners are very tempted to try to repeat the operation. They go to enormous lengths to get the lead into the North hand again so that they can trump another heart. But have they achieved anything? Hardly, for they have taken two tricks and now have only four tricks left. Total, six tricks – exactly the number of tricks with which they started. What is worse, if you have started with something like:

♠4 3 2

♠A K Q J 10

(where you have begun with only five tricks) and you go out of your way to trump twice in the South hand, you will have achieved very little – you still have only five tricks in all – and you may run into difficulties when you try to extract their trumps. Remember, you have only three left in your hand and one of the opponents may still hold four. And yet there is this fatal attraction about "trumping in" which is difficult to resist.

Let us go back to the original suit of:

♠4 3 2

♠A K Q J 10 9

and suppose that there had been the chance of trumping something in the *North* hand. Can you see how this works? Suppose that you had started with:

♠4 3 2
♡2

♠A K Q J 10 9
♡5 4 3

"WHEN I SAY DRAW TRUMPS, DON'T TAKE ME TOO LITERALLY."

Again spades are trumps, again you have six easy tricks and again the opponents lead hearts. You trump the second round in dummy and this is an *extra* trick, for you still have your original six winners. With any luck you will be able to do the same thing again – get the lead into the South hand in order to lead the last heart and trump that one. Result? Two extra tricks and South still has his six winners.

It seems as though trumping in dummy is always a good idea but bridge is a funny game. It is rare that you can say "always" and it is rare that you can say "never". Just imagine that this is your trump suit:

♡Q J 7 6 5

♡A K 4 2

If you just look at the tricks then things are easy – you have five winners for by the time you have played off the Ace, King, Queen and Jack neither opponent can have any cards left. Fine but now suppose that you had the chance of trumping one card in dummy. One trick, but now only four left and nothing gained. Try it the other way round – suppose that you had the chance of trumping something in your own hand? A trick and the partnership still has five tricks to come. In other words, an extra trick but this time by ruffing in your own hand, apparently contradicting all our earlier ideas. Not quite: now we can put things more clearly. You gain tricks if you can ruff in the *short* trump hand (the one with fewer cards) and suddenly things are upside down. Usually it is dummy that is the short trump hand but in this example it is declarer that has fewer trumps. A ruff in declarer's hand now pays off, and everything seems upside down. But this only happens about 10% of the time – usually declarer will have at least as many trumps as dummy.

What we have been talking about so far links in very closely with what is always a big problem when you are playing a hand with a trump suit – should you draw the opponents trumps as soon as possible? In other words make sure that you win tricks with your high trump cards before they have the chance to score any tricks with their little ones? The trouble is that the answer is not always obvious. There is an old saying dating from whist-playing days that "There is many a man sleeping on the Embankment because he forgot to draw trumps". But it can work the other way as well. Suppose that we go back to our old friend:

♠4 3 2
♡5

♠A K Q J 10
♡4 3 2

Five certain tricks with spades as trumps but suppose that your opponents aren't kind enough to lead hearts for you? You get the lead, perhaps with a diamond or a club, and if you draw trumps you will need to play at least three rounds. This will have an unfortunate side effect – all dummy's trumps will go as well! So when the opponents gain the lead later, they will be able to take three heart tricks. You could have done something about it by playing hearts yourself *before* drawing trumps. You take your two ruffs on the table (extra tricks, as we have seen) and only then draw the opponents' trumps. It is always something to look out for – a side-suit shortage in the dummy and a few spare trumps to go with it. Everybody notices a void and usually takes full advantage, most people feel that a singleton is going to help, but what about a doubleton in dummy? This is often overlooked. Think of a pair of suits like this:

♠4 3 2
♡6 5

♠A K Q J 10
♡4 3 2

There is an extra trick there, but not if you draw trumps first. If you need that extra trick you have got to give up two tricks in hearts first.

With – I hope! – a better idea of how trumps should be used we will look at a few hands and decide how to play them. Two bits of advice before you start looking at them – (1) Count your certain winners or at least try to do so. (2) Ask yourself whether this is a hand where you want to draw trumps or not. At least you will now have some sort of a plan in mind before you tackle the play. Perhaps, though, the most important thing to keep in mind is that *you shouldn't rush to play to the first trick.* If you are in Five Diamonds, needing eleven tricks, there is no prize for making the first ten tricks quickly and losing the last three slowly. Far better to think a little *first* and then you may come to all the tricks that you need.

Time now for a few hands to show the different ways of using the trumps. Try this:

♠6
♡7 5 3
♢J 8 5 3
♣A K Q J 10

♠8 7 4
♡A K Q J 10
♢K 6 2
♣7 4

Reasonably enough you end up in a contract of Four Hearts against which West leads a small club. With little choice you play one of dummy's top clubs and it wins the trick when East follows suit. You need ten tricks for your contract – how many do you make if you draw all the missing trumps? Right, the required ten tricks with five top hearts followed by the rest of the winning clubs. It all looks too easy and that's how you play it so that nothing can go wrong. But there is a little trap built in to this deal. Doesn't it look tempting to remember how trumps can work for you and prepare the ground by giving up a spade as soon as you get in? Then you may be able to ruff one or even two spades in dummy, then draw trumps, then run the remaining clubs.

Oh, dear. Several things can go wrong with this plan and they all might happen because you hadn't counted your certain winners. Just try it out – lead a low spade at trick 2. Here is one possible danger if you find the cards like this:

"THERE IS MANY A MAN SLEEPING ON THE EMBANKMENT BECAUSE HE DID DRAW TRUMPS."
NEWS
NEWS
BEDTIME STORIES
HOT WATER BOTTLE

| | North | |
|---|---|---|
| | ♠6<br>♡7 5 3<br>♢J 8 5 3<br>♣A K Q J 10 | |
| ♠K J 10 3<br>♡9 6 4<br>♢A Q 10 4<br>♣9 5 | N<br>W E<br>S | ♠A Q 9 5 2<br>♡8 2<br>♢9 7<br>♣8 6 3 2 |
| | ♠8 7 4<br>♡A K Q J 10<br>♢K 6 2<br>♣7 4 | |

East wins the spade lead with his Ace and pushes through a diamond. It doesn't matter what you try – West will win tricks with his Queen and Ace and lead a third diamond which East will ruff. That will be four tricks for the defenders and there will be no way for you to make ten tricks and your contract with only nine cards.

Perhaps you think that I have arranged the East-West cards in the worst possible way. Not at all – I could also have given West a singleton club and now the defenders are able to collect a ruff in clubs instead. And even if neither of the opponents can trump anything, suppose that whoever wins the spade plays a club back. Now there is a new problem, of your own making, for if you draw trumps now you are left with no clubs in hand and can't get at dummy's winners. If instead you try to take the winning clubs first you can be quite sure that someone will trump. There is a very clear moral here. If you have enough top winners, draw trumps!

Change the scene just a little by weakening dummy's clubs:

♠6
♡7 5 3
♢J 8 5 3
♣A K 5 3 2

♠8 7 4
♡A K Q J 10
♢K 6 2
♣7 4

You still reach Four Hearts and when you see dummy you realise that your partner has done too much bidding. That is one of the features of a partnership game like bridge – you always mentally blame partner if things go wrong for you rarely make a mistake. (Or so it seems to every player I have ever known! To keep harmony I think that there should be only two things that you ever say to partner after a hand. One is "Well done!" if the outcome has been satisfactory, the other is "Bad luck!" after he has done something terrible. In this way you will make many friends over the years over the table. . . .) Sorry, we seem to have wandered away from the hand.

You get the lead of a low club and, again, you must lean back, relax and count your winners. First, if you draw trumps you will make five hearts, only two clubs and (on your good days) a trick in diamonds to bring you a total of eight tricks.

"THERE IS MANY A MAN SLEEPING ON THE EMBANKMENT BECAUSE HE DIDN'T DRAW TRUMPS."

That is no good so think of the possibility of not drawing trumps. It is now essential to give up a spade trick at the first opportunity. Just as before, they might manage to take two diamond tricks and a ruff or even trump one of your club winners but these are chances that you now have to take. So you win the opening lead and give up a trick in spades. If your opponents can't do anything terrible to you, what might they try? Give it a moment's thought. . .

* * *

This is an interesting idea and well worth noting. If you are a defender and declarer doesn't draw trumps it is likely that he has a good reason for leaving dummy's trumps alone. If he doesn't play them it may be a good idea for you to do something about it before he can use dummy's trumps independently.

It sounds good advice but take it with a pinch of salt! If declarer gives the impression of knowing what he is doing, fine. But against some declarers (and you will meet them) the explanation for his failure to draw trumps may have been that he just didn't think about it – or had forgotten what trumps were – and now by playing the suit yourself you might be pushing him back in the right direction.

However, on the deal we are considering East does win the first spade lead and pushes back a trump. For all he knows you might still have three losing spades left in your hand and need all three of dummy's trumps to look after them. Now you have only two trumps left on the table. They have found the best defence but you are not dead yet. You win the trump in hand, ruff one of your losing spades in dummy and consider what to do next. You would like to ruff your last losing spade but unfortunately the lead is in dummy at the moment. How can you get it into your hand? A trump lead solves this problem but takes dummy's last trump away before you are able to use it.

There is only one practical way to go about things. You must cash dummy's remaining high club and ruff a club in your own hand. It doesn't give you an extra trick for you were always going to score with your top heart but it does give you the lead where you want it. Now you can lead your last spade, trump it in dummy and find yourself looking at nine tricks. A big improvement but you are not there yet.

Whatever you do, with your nine tricks in sight, don't waste time in trumping another club. That was only an emergency measure to get the lead where you wanted it. As you have the lead in dummy for the last time you must try and take advantage of it by leading a low diamond towards the King. If the Ace is well placed for you – with East – you are likely to make the tenth trick that you need for your contract. If West turns up with the Ace of diamonds and you end with only nine tricks you can concentrate on thinking dark thoughts about your partner's optimistic bidding but at least you will have tried.

Let us still suppose that you are in Four Hearts but that this time you have some different material with which to work:

♠3
♡Q J 7 6 4
◇A 6 3
♣9 5 2

♠9 5 2
♡A K 10 8 5
◇K 8 4
♣A 3

Against your heart contract (target – ten tricks) West leads the Queen of diamonds and, as usual, you take stock. If you win and rattle off everything in sight you end with five hearts, two diamonds and a club – only eight tricks. Right, is this one of those hands where you have to give up a spade immediately, planning to ruff two diamonds in dummy? No, here we have come to a half-way house. Your side has enough trumps to sink a battleship and there is no reason at all why trumps shouldn't be drawn immediately. At worst three rounds will be needed (after all, there are only three missing) to draw all the trumps and there will still be two left in dummy to look after the two losing spades. *Remember*, draw trumps unless there is a good reason not to!

If you forget to draw trumps and make a start on spades you will make your contract *most* of the time but every once in a while they will manage to trump your Ace of clubs or your remaining high diamond. Unlikely? Yes, but there was no need to take the risk.

Try another type of hand. This time the contract is Four Spades (everyone gets bored with playing in Four Hearts . . .):

♠A J 9 3
♡7
◇A 10 7 4
♣A 8 6 3

| West | | East |
|---|---|---|
| ♠5 | N | ♠8 7 6 2 |
| ♡Q 10 8 5 | W E | ♡K J 3 2 |
| ◇K Q J | | ◇9 5 |
| ♣K 10 7 5 4 | S | ♣Q J 2 |

♠K Q 10 4
♡A 9 6 4
◇8 6 3 2
♣9

After some aggressive bidding South is the declarer (the North-South values are a little thin on the ground!) and West leads the King of diamonds. Think it through as logically as you can. Your thought processes might go like this:

*Stage One.* If I just take everything in sight I will end with four spades and three Aces – seven tricks?

*Stage Two.* Is it as bad as it seems? Probably three rounds of trumps will be enough to draw all of their little ones. That will leave me with one trump in each hand and it shouldn't be difficult to make them separately – eight tricks.

*Stage Three.* Anything else to come in? Nothing from hearts or clubs but if the missing diamonds break no worse than 3–2 I can establish an extra trick in the suit. Grand total, if *everything* has gone well, nine tricks and that is no good if I am in Four Spades.

*Stage Four*. Abandon the plan of drawing trumps straight away? I can see that it doesn't work.

*Stage Five*. Next I consider the idea of trumping my three

losing hearts in dummy before drawing trumps. It looks fine but there is a practical difficulty. I will find it harder and harder to get the lead back into my own hand without using up my own trumps.

*Stage Six.* Give up?

*Stage Seven*. I never give up. Instead I will try a new idea – a plan of campaign that we call a cross-ruff. Think of the effect of making no attempt at all to draw their trumps but concentrating on making *as many of ours as possible separately.* Suddenly light dawns and life becomes a pleasure. Try it out! The narrative is terse but cross out the cards as you go and You will see what is happening. Here goes. ♢A, ♣A, club ruff, ♡A, heart ruff, club ruff, heart ruff, club ruff, heart ruff. If you haven't lost your breath you will see that I have already taken nine tricks and I still have the Ace and King of trumps left. To my annoyance I can't make them separately but I am home and dry with ten tricks. At the end East will have three trumps left and he will be able to amuse himself by trumping his partner's winning diamonds.

For a successful cross-ruff you need plenty of trumps in both hands together with a suit facing a shortage and a shortage facing a suit. The hand above was a perfect example – in both hands the suit headed by the Ace was faced by a singleton. Sometimes you have a little work to do first. You may have a doubleton (instead of a singleton) in one hand and before the cross-ruff can start you have to concede a trick.

A final thought. If you are a *defender* and feel that the other side are going to play the hand on a cross-ruff, what do you lead? Quite right, a trump. At least that will be two of their trumps that they can't make separately! It may not always work out well but it is certainly an idea to bear in mind.

# Chapter 11

## OPENING LEADS

Perhaps the part of the game about which the most questions are asked is the problem of finding an opening lead – the card that starts off the play to each hand. Can you see why the problem is so difficult? You have only your own thirteen cards and the bidding to guide you! Once the lead has been made and dummy appears then everyone will be able to see at least twenty-six cards and indeed, as the play goes on, more and more cards appear and – with any luck – decisions become easier.

There is another point too. Whereas it is often easy to say 'This is the right bid' or 'It is correct to draw trumps,' it is much rarer that you are completely convinced that you are finding the best lead. All we can do in this chapter is to *suggest* a few ideas for you to think about – some Do's and Don'ts to use as guidelines.

You would like your opening lead to be two things:

1. Constructive
2. Safe

By constructive we mean starting to do something useful for your side – not necessarily winning a trick but *establishing* a winner or winners in either your hand or partners'.

And by safe we mean not letting the opposition make a trick to which they were not entitled. Of course, that is not the same as letting them make an Ace – they were almost certainly going to enjoy a trick with it sooner or later – but think of a suit like this:

|  | 4 3 |  |
|---|---|---|
| A Q 8 7 6 |  | J 10 9 5 |
|  | K 2 |  |

If West leads this suit, either by leading a low card, or by playing off his Ace, South's King will become a winner. An undeserved winner, too, for if South had had to play this suit for himself he would not have got anywhere – all he could have tried was low towards the King, failing when West turned up with the Ace.

What then is a lead which is both constructive and safe? The best example is when you have a suit that starts off with a sequence of at least three touching cards – perhaps:

|  |  |
|---|---|
|  | A K Q 2 |
| or | K Q J 10 4 |
| or | Q J 10 7 |
| or | J 10 9 3 |

If you have been lucky enough to have been dealt a useful sequence, you don't want to ruin the effect by leading a low card. For example, if a suit is distributed like this:

K 5 4

Q J 10 7 8 6 2

A 9 3

and you were on lead with the West hand, it would be foolish to lead the 7. Dummy plays low, your partner can't do much about it and declarer wins a cheap trick with his nine, with the Ace and King still in reserve. He makes three tricks instead of two. If instead West had led one of his honours, declarer would have had to use up one of his high cards. When West gets in again he leads another high card and now the Ace or King (whichever is left) has to take the trick. Result? West is left with a winner whatever the contract may be, and if it happens to be no-trumps, he will even have an extra winner with his seven.

Good, that is stage one. If you have a sequence of touching high cards you lead one of them. But which one? As far as you are concerned they are all the same value. If you have the King, the Queen and the Jack in a suit, your Jack is just as likely to take a trick as your King. The trouble is that bridge is a partnership game, this cannot be emphasised too strongly. *You have a partner who you want to help rather than mystify*. Just suppose that with K Q J 3 in a suit you lead the Queen. Is not partner, with perhaps A 5 4 in the suit, going to wonder who holds the King? He may end up by playing the Ace and now your side will have managed two high cards on one trick – clearly a complete waste for you like to make high cards *separately*.

Try the effect of leading the King. Now there is no incentive at all for partner to waste his Ace, for he can see that your King is working just as well.

Stick to this idea then – from a sequence you *lead* the top card. If you always do it and your partner always does it *you know where you are*. And that is a big thing in bridge. Try it out. Partner leads the Queen and this is what you can see:

7 6 5

Q A 9 8 4 3

Who has got the King? Not partner, for he has led the Queen. Not you or dummy – you can see that! Therefore declarer (South) has the missing King and you should play your Ace in case the King is all by itself (a singleton).

Although we discussed the matter elsewhere, it is worth thinking about a slightly different problem, for the contrast is rather helpful. As we have suggested, with Q J 10 9 you *lead* the Queen. But suppose that you are sitting in the East position, your partner has led the 2 and this is what you can see in the suit?

7 6 5

2 Q J 10 9

?

Which card should you play? It is no good saying, rather feebly, that 'It doesn't matter, they are all the same.' You must remember *partner*. Suppose that this was the full suit:

7 6 5

K 4 3 2 Q J 10 9

A 8

Now it is important to go the other way. After your partner has led a suit, or if you are winning a trick in the fourth position at the table, you do the best that you can but you play the *lowest* card that will do all the work necessary So here you contribute the nine. Again you may ask what possible difference it can make, but think of it from partner's side. What can he see if you play the Queen and declarer wins with the Ace?

7 6 5

K 4 3 2 Q ?

A ?

Poor old West is left wondering who has got the Jack, ten and nine. But if you had contributed the nine on the first trick and this had forced declarer's Ace, he would know that you held the Queen, Jack and ten as well. Otherwise why did declarer waste his Ace if he could have won the trick much more cheaply?

We seem to have wandered a little from opening leads, but never mind. At least you can now see the logic of *leading* the Queen from Q J 10 9 and attempting to win a trick if your partner leads the suit, with the nine. And this is something that should become absolutely second nature to you, no matter how far the hand has progressed. To take an extreme case – you get to trick 12 (only two cards to go) – and you are on lead with ♠Q J. Lead the Queen! But if your partner leads a low spade and dummy plays low, contribute the Jack. Of course it doesn't really matter too much at this very late stage – just get into the habit of doing it ALL the time and you won't forget and get it wrong at a time when it might really matter.

The main idea that we have established so far about leading is that a suit headed by a sequence is usually an excellent choice. It is both *constructive* and *safe*, if you remember our keywords, provided we choose the top card. Of course, you don't always get dealt a sequence, but you might find yourself with a suit that looks like:

A K J 3
or K Q 10 5
or Q J 9 3

they don't start off with full sequences but they each start with two in succession, then a gap, then the next card. They have been called 'near sequences' or '2½ sequences' but neither phrase is very memorable, so you won't find them in the glossary . . . .

If you lead just the same card that you would have chosen

from a full sequence of at least three touching cards, you will still be making a good *constructive* lead. The only trouble is that your lead is no longer quite as *safe*. For example:

K 10 3

Q J 9 7          8 6 5

A 4 2

You lead the Queen, South wins in hand with the Ace and later leads a low card from hand to finesse dummy's ten. Now declarer makes three tricks in the suit instead of just the Ace and King to which he would have been restricted if you hadn't opened the suit. Can you see the difference? If declarer tries to do it all by himself, starting the suit by leading low from the South hand, you can put in the Jack to stop him scoring with dummy's ten. But if you had led the Queen initially, you are suddenly helpless.

Mind you, it was rather unlucky to find your lead costing a trick. Look at all the things that had to go wrong! First, if partner had held *any* of the Ace, King or ten there would have been no danger of giving away the extra trick. Secondly, declarer and dummy must both have exactly one of the Ace and King. Thirdly, dummy has got to hold the ten! So quite a lot has to go wrong before the lead works badly. It is worth while for you to think out how a lead from K Q 10 2 might work out badly. . . .

If you can't see how the recommended lead of the King might cost, picture a suit like this:

J 5 4

K Q 10 2      8 7 6

A 9 3

If the first trick goes King, four, six and Ace, then declarer can organise a second trick by leading low towards the Jack. But if West had never led the suit at all, South couldn't possibly have come to anything more than his Ace.

Right, in reserve you have one excellent lead (a full sequence) and one good lead (a near sequence). The trouble is that you don't always get dealt a suit like that. Far more often you find yourself inspecting a suit that looks like Q 10 7 5 2 and you decide to lead it. (Of course you don't have to lead this particular suit, but suppose that you *do* decide to lead it?) It is standard practice to lead the *fourth highest* – that is the fourth best, counting from the top, in this case the five.

You may ask why. There are technical reasons for choosing this particular card from a suit but the best practical reason is that everyone else does it and will expect you to do it. (Don't be like Johnny, whose proud mother watched him marching past in a parade and remarked, 'There's our Johnny. He's the only one in step!') There are certainly one or two simple points that show why fourth highest is a good idea. For example, against no-trumps, when you normally expect a player to lead a long suit, your partner leads the two. How many cards did he start with in that suit? Right, exactly four. If the two is his fourth highest card and (clearly) his lowest, he can't have any more cards. And if you know how many cards partner has got and you can see how many cards both you and dummy hold, you will be able to work out how many cards declarer has got. That can't be bad, and you gradually start to build up a picture of the declarer's hand.

So far we have made no distinction between the two sorts of contract – no-trumps and contracts where one of the four suits is trumps. You still lead the top of a sequence or near-sequence and if you decide to lead a long broken suit you choose the fourth highest. However, just let us think about our reasons for wanting to lead from Q 10 7 5 2. Against no-trumps our motive is that we must attempt to get our long suit working. It is rare for you to have been dealt enough Aces and Kings to defeat them in top tricks; far more often you must establish tricks in your long suit. With this example you hope that your partner can produce one (or even two) high cards in the suit and you can drive out whatever guard or stopper declarer has there. Once that has gone, with any luck, you might come to four tricks.

But when there is a trump suit, although you lead the same card, your ambition is much more limited. It is unlikely to be of much use to establish winners for your low cards, for they will simply be trumped in dummy or in declarer's hand. Perhaps the best that you could hope for is a suit distributed like this:

| | | |
|---|---|---|
| | 8 6 4 | |
| Q 10 7 5 2 | | K 3 |
| | A J 9 | |

Your lead of the five goes to the four, King and Ace; now you sit and wait with your Q 10 poised over South's J 9. As soon as your partner gets in with *some other suit* and returns your lead, you will be able to take two tricks. But it only needs, say, one more card in your partner's hand and one less card in dummy and you will only have succeeded in building up one more trick.

So that is the big difference when you lead from a long suit – against no-trumps you hope to bring in most of the suit, against a trump contract you only have hopes of one or two of your top cards working. It hasn't changed your lead but suppose instead that you had started with:

A K 7 5 2

Against no-trumps you lead your fourth highest. You expect declarer, who has bid no-trumps, to have a guard in the suit but equally you hope that this guard will have to be used up on your lead. Perhaps:

| | J 9 3 | |
|---|---|---|
| A K 7 5 2 | | 8 4 |
| | Q 10 6 | |

Certainly declarer wins the first trick but, no matter whether it is you or your partner who gets in next, you now have four winners ready to run.

Change the scene a little and imagine that there is a trump suit. With your Ace and King you only expect to make two tricks – there is no future for your low cards anymore – and so with this holding you would lead the Ace. Look on the bright side! In the example given you will not only make the Ace and the King but your partner will be able to trump the next one that you lead and declarer won't come to any trick at all in the suit. What would have happened if you had absent-mindedly led the fourth highest against a suit contract? South would win with the ten and draw trumps. Now one of your sides possible tricks would have run away.

Giving you advance warning that it is a little bit of a trap question, what would you lead from a suit of:

A 10 7 5 2

The first trap is that we haven't said what the contract is! Against no-trumps you haven't got a care in the world and you lead the five. But suppose that one of the suits is trumps? There's the second trap. When you are defending, your Aces are best used to win tricks containing Kings and Queens belonging to your opponents. If you *lead* Aces, you tend to collect two's and three's and establish tricks for their Kings and Queens. Your main excuse for leading an Ace is that you have the King as well! You may ask, then, what is wrong with leading the five, just as you would against no-trumps? Well, when there is a trump suit it always seems to turn out that either declarer or dummy has the King all by itself. The lone King wins and, later on, your Ace is trumped. Yet if you *lead* the Ace, the King is never alone and turns into an undeserved trick for declarer. You may think that I am exaggerating the risks but leading a suit like this works out so badly, so often, that it is a good idea never to lead it when you are making the opening lead against a suit contract by your opponents. In fact, this can almost be stated as a golden rule of opening leads – 'When there is a trump suit, *never* underlead an Ace.' By 'underlead' of course, we mean 'leading a low card from a suit which contains' but it is simpler and shorter to put it in one word.

While we are on the subject of leads that work out badly, there are some others that are absolute horrors, such as any short suit containing a couple of honours such as A Q 2, A J 2, K J 2, Q 10 2, K 10 2, and so on. You do so much better, with suits like these, to sit and wait. Take an extreme case – suppose that you had started with A Q 10 in a suit – where would you like to be sitting at the table? We don't mean North, South etc., but would you prefer to be on lead, the second player, the third player or the last player to a trick in this suit? If you lead your Queen it may lose to the King and your ten to the Jack, but if only you are allowed to be in the fourth seat you are much better placed. If it happens to you twice, you will have three tricks in the suit instead of perhaps only one if you had felt the urge to lead the suit.

So far, quite a lot of 'don'ts'. However, when you are at work against no-trumps, you do normally choose a long suit – top of a sequence if you have got it, fourth highest if the suit is broken. But against a suit contract there is a new possibility – that of leading a *short* suit. Ideally a singleton, for if your partner has the Ace you will be at an advantage immediately – he takes his Ace, returns the suit and you have the chance to make a trick with a low trump that otherwise you may never have made. So with:

♠A 4 3
♡Q 10 7 5 2
◇J 9 7 4
♣4

if your opponent had bid 1NT – 3NT you would lead ♡5, but if they had bid One Spade – Four Spades then the singleton four of Clubs would be a much more attractive proposition. Look on the bright side – even if partner hasn't got the Ace of Clubs, the declarer won't be able to draw trumps without you getting in with the Ace of Spades. And when you do, there is a fair chance that you will be able to give your partner the lead with one of the red suits and still take a ruff in clubs before your trumps are drawn.

Don't get the idea that leading a singleton is always good. Suppose, still defending against Four Spades, you held:

♠K Q J
♡Q 10 7 5 2
◇J 9 7 4
♣4

Here, with two certain *natural* trump tricks, you really don't want to trump anything, as nothing *extra* will come in. But when your spades were A 4 3 you could only hope for one trick, unless you were able to ruff something with one of your low trumps.

Another possibility, usually a little less likely to produce results than a singleton, is to lead a doubleton. It can go well – sometimes partner has both the Ace and the King, sometimes partner may have the Ace and Queen sitting over the

King in dummy. Even if there is no immediate ruff, you can sometimes organise one before all of your trumps are drawn. When you do decide to lead a doubleton, you always lead the higher of your two cards. So against Four Spades with:

♠A 4 3
♡Q 10 7 5
♢J 9 7 4
♣8 4

you *could* lead ♡5 or ♢4, but ♣8 would perhaps be a more attractive choice.

Finally, you often find yourself in the position of leading a suit that contains complete rubbish, with no honour card at all. Say ♣8 7 2. If you lead this suit the card to choose is the eight and we call this a 'top-of-nothing' lead. It is not particularly constructive and usually your reason for choosing the lead is that everything else looks even less attractive! At least the lead is usually safe. If you had started with:

♠A Q 7
♡J 5 4 2
♢8 7 2
♣K J 9

and found yourself, as West, on lead after the bidding:

| *SOUTH* | *WEST* | *NORTH* | *EAST* |
|---|---|---|---|
| 1 ♡ | No bid | 1 NT | No bid |
| 2 ♡ | No bid | No bid | No bid |

how should you think? Take it suit by suit. Spades? Unattractive, for you have a short suit with two honours and this, as we have seen, is a suit where it usually pays to sit and wait. Very much the same is true of the clubs and you would prefer to leave these alone too. Hearts? Yes, they are trumps, but that is not the reason why you don't want to lead them. You have a guard, a likely trick in the suit which (more often than not) you will make. Yet if you lead trumps here your trick might easily disappear. Suppose the hearts lie like this:

| | ♡9 6 | |
|---|---|---|
| ♡J 5 4 2 | | ♡7 3 |
| | ♡A K Q 10 8 | |

If you sit tight you will eventually score with ♡J: if you lead the suit you won't!

The solution then to your problem is to lead a diamond. It is not a dynamic lead but it should be reasonably safe. Which card? Top-of-nothing – the eight.

The pattern of leads is starting to fall into place now. You may still find it difficult to pick the right suit, but at least you know which card to lead. And the size of your card often gets over an important message to partner.

(1) If you lead an honour, he can judge that your suit starts with a sequence.
(2) If you lead a low-looking card he can judge that you have led fourth highest.

(3) If you lead a high-looking card he can judge that you have led top-of-nothing.

Of course, it doesn't always work (singletons and doubletons come in all sorts of sizes!) but you will be suggesting the type of suit that you have led from quite a lot of the time. Try one or two little problems – in each case your partner leads the six of spades against a contract of Four Hearts, and this is what you can see in spades:

(1)

♠K 5 4 3

♠6 led ♠A Q 2

♠?

What do you make of the lead? It can't be top-of nothing because *you can see all the lower cards*. It is unlikely to be a singleton for then declarer would have started with five spades and you would have been sure to have heard something about that in the bidding. So all that remains is that he has led fourth highest.

(2)

♠K J 8

♠6 led ♠A Q 10 7

♠?

What do you make of the lead? It can't be fourth highest for there is only one card higher than the six that you cannot see. Again, it is unlikely to be a singleton (as declarer would have five) so the lead is either a doubleton or top-of-nothing.

(3)

♠K 8 5

♠6 led ♠A Q 7 2

♠?

What do you make of the lead? Unlikely to be a singleton, could be top of nothing, but could it be fourth highest? There are, after all, three cards higher than the six that you can't see. But think on! The three missing cards are the Jack, ten and nine, and with a suit starting ♠J 10 9 6, what would West have led? Right, the Jack, and as he hasn't, his lead *can't* be fourth highest.

To repeat, you won't always read your partner's lead correctly but you will have a number of clues – dummy's cards, your cards, the card declarer plays on the first trick, the bidding. At all times bear in mind that *there is a big difference between the fourth highest and the top of nothing!*

Before we wind up this chapter on opening leads we must think of one thing that may, indeed *should*, influence our choice. Sometimes our partner has bid! And if he has done so there are two good reasons why you should lead his suit rather than one of your own. First, it may easily be the best lead. Second, *it keeps your partner happy!* He doesn't feel that he has been wasting his efforts in telling you what he would like led. Nothing is more irritating than to make a rather sporting bid to suggest a lead, escape unpunished in the bidding, lean back tired but happy, wait for partner to lead your suit and then to your horror, find that partner is *thinking*! What can he be thinking about? You have *told* him what you would like led! Finally partner comes out of his trance and leads some horrible suit of his own in which you haven't the slightest interest. It is at moments like this that people are tempted to give up bridge. . . .

Good, problem solved. If partner has bid, you will lead his suit. Well, to be fair, there are sometimes excuses for doing other things. But they have to be pretty good excuses, like not having any cards at all in his suit, or perhaps (having heard partner bid spades) finding yourself on lead against 3NT with ♢A K Q J 10 in your own hand when, you feel, there might be a good case for taking them first and defeating their contract.

Now, if you are always going to lead partner's suit, it means that you may have to lead from suits that otherwise you might not have opened up. Singleton – well, you have no choice there! Doubletons – you have got used to leading the higher card already. But if partner has bid the suit you will now look at A x, K x, and Q x with more interest. Normally you wouldn't have led the suit (it would be a little like the Charge of the Light Brigade!) but when partner has bid it, off you go, lead the higher.

With four or more cards in partner's suit it is easy stuff – fourth highest as usual. So we lead the 5 from Q 10 7 5 2, the 3 from K 9 7 3 and so on. One exception. Against suit contracts if you hold the Ace of your partner's bid suit, lead it, regardless of how many other cards you hold in that suit.

However, there is a new problem. If you have three cards headed by an honour, what should you do? Perhaps K 7 3 or Q 8 5 or 10 5 2? In the normal run of things you would not have led a suit like this but if partner has bid it you feel obliged to do so. (We know two old gentlemen who played bridge together for 30 years. Then one of them didn't lead his partner's suit and, not only have they not played in partnership for the last twenty years – they haven't spoken to each other! Mind you, there was some excuse – leading partner's suit would have led to 6NT redoubled and vulnerable going six down – 3400 points! – instead of making with an overtrick – 2660 points the other way!

Sorry, we have wandered from the point. With three cards headed by an honour (and remember the ten counts as an honour) lead your lowest card. So, K 7 **3**, Q 6 **5**, 10 5 **2**.

In a way, this fits in well with our general thinking about leads. Low cards suggest something of interest in the suit, high (ish) cards suggest top-of-nothing and no better values.

As a post script, you may have heard the catch-phrase, 'Lead the highest card you have in your partner's suit'. Forget it, unless you have only one or two cards. Just look at this suit:

| | ♠6 3 | |
|---|---|---|
| ♠Q 8 5 | | ♠A 10 9 7 4 |
| | ♠K J 2 | |

South is in a no-trump contract and East has bid spades. Try it out. How many tricks in the suit does declarer make if West mistakenly leads ♠Q? And how many does he make if West correctly leads the 5?

Work it out, work it out! The good advice is all above and you can now see why.

# Chapter 12

## THE SHAPE OF THINGS TO COME

You have come a long way now. You can open the bidding, respond and rebid. You know when it is a good idea to play in no-trumps rather than choose your best suit. You have met most of the different ways of building up tricks both in no-trumps and in suit contracts. You know how a partnership uses its bids to decide whether they have enough between them to make it worth their while bidding game and you have some idea of scoring. With this base you can start to play an enjoyable game and will probably be able to understand a good few of the articles that you come across in newspaper columns.

What is more, you will have a sound foundation to read more advanced books on the game. This one doesn't pretend for a moment to be anything more than a "starter". There have been literally thousands of bridge books written, on both the bidding and play, in English alone (the international language of bridge bidding, by the way; if you play in an international tournament in, say, Venezuala, all the bids will be made in English). You will find most of the other books far more complicated. Even if they set out to instruct beginners, most of them get much too far into the theory of the game and put off their readers before they have really started. Don't think that you will never play well, persevere with the simple stuff first. Later on, with a little experience,

"THE BIDDING WENT
TWO CLUBS, PASS, PASS, PASS."
FIRST AID

will be the time to start thinking about a few of the ideas that I will sketch out now. And, believe me, it is only going to be a sketch of a few lines to tell you what to look out for or ask about if you decide to push on with bridge. Think of it as an end of term reading list! Not compulsory but you will find that it will help. No details, just enough to whet your appetite. . .

(1) An opening bid of Two Clubs (not an overcall, not a response, just an opening bid) is usually played to mean that you have a huge hand. I don't mean more than thirteen cards of course, just the sort of hand that wants to be in a game even if partner has absolutely nothing. For example, you might be the dealer with

♠A K J 6 5
♡A K J 5 4
◇A 4
♣A

Enormous, but if you open One Spade or One Heart your partner may easily pass with less than six points. You want practically nothing for game but you can't just close your eyes and open Four Spades or Four Hearts. It would be so easy to choose the wrong suit. Start with Two Clubs – a conventional bid, not necessarily showing anything at all in clubs but insisting on game – and you will have time to tell partner about both of your suits and see which one he prefers.

(2) An opening bid of Two of a suit, other than clubs which (as we have seen) has a special meaning. It suggests that you are *near* game in your own hand but can't quite insist on it. For example, with:

♠A K Q 10 8 7
♡A 7 6
◇3
♣A Q 5

you will make a game if partner holds as little as:

♠6 5 3
♡K 8 5 3
◇8 7 4 2
♣9 3

but you won't make game if he has *complete* rubbish. Solution? Open Two Spades.

(3) There is a bonus for bidding and making a small slam (twelve tricks) or a bigger bonus for bidding and making a grand slam (all thirteen tricks). One of the devices that a lot of players use is the *Blackwood* convention. It is a bid of 4NT half-way through the auction which simply asks how many Aces partner holds. (Replies, Five Clubs – no Aces, Five Diamonds – one Ace, Five Hearts – two Aces, . . . You get the idea?). Now of course, it is one thing to know a convention and another when to use it sensibly. That is part of your further education!

(4) Using your high cards when you are defending – always a problem because you can't see your partner's hand and you haven't got very many high cards to play around with. . . .

(5) Signalling and discarding. You might think that the defenders are each fighting a lone battle. Not so; they have ways of getting messages across to each other that suggest whether they like partner's activities (for example, choice of

lead) or not. I don't mean the scowl and the sharp intake of breath nor the pleased smile and the nod that some players have been known to use. No, there are more legitimate and more reliable methods available. Very much the same is true when you have to throw things away; often a horror but if you can tell partner something while you are doing it all may not be lost.

(6) There is another big problem – joining in the bidding after the opponents have opened. Suddenly things take on a slightly different slant. Once the other side have opened, your chances of making a game are very much reduced. Bids, then, have a much more defensive character than opening bids. For example, if the player on my right opened One Heart and I joined in with One Spade, I wouldn't expect my partner to place me with a full opening bid. A good suit, yes, but not necessarily a full thirteen points. If you have got a good hand, there is something called the take-out double which often comes to your aid.

If you think that these are the only areas of the game that we haven't had a chance to discuss, then look on the bright side. There are a great many more. Watch this space . . . Perhaps 12+ Bridge will come next. . .

"PITY CYNTHIA NEVER LEARNT TO PLAY BRIDGE."

# GLOSSARY

*Above the line.* Points scored which, for one reason or another, do not count towards a game.

*Auction.* (See Bidding)

*Balanced hand.* A hand with no long suits and no short suits. Typically a 4-3-3-3 or 4-4-3-2 distribution.

*Below the line.* Points scored for bidding and making a contract, so counting towards a game.

*Bidding.* The 'discussion' that helps a partnership decide what is their best trump suit and how many tricks they want to try to make.

*Contract.* When a player makes a bid he contracts to make a certain number of tricks with his partner. The last suit or no-trump call in the auction determines the final contract.

And, of course, the full name of the game is Contract Bridge.

*Deal.* To deal is to distribute the cards, one at a time, clockwise, to the four players. But when we talk about *a* deal we mean the full collection of four hands, each of thirteen cards, after they have been dealt.

*Declarer.* The member of the partnership who first bids the suit that finally becomes trumps. If you like, the player who 'invented' the idea of using the suit as trumps.

*Discard.* When you can't follow suit and cannot or do not want to trump, the card that you play, (from some other suit), is called a discard and has no chance of winning the trick.

*Double.* A bid that suggests you don't think that the opponents can make their contract. It has the effect of doubling their score if they make it, and increasing yours substantially if they fail.

*Doubleton.* Exactly two cards in a suit.

*Dummy.* The partner of the declarer, but only after the opening lead is made does he put his cards down and become the dummy.

*Finesse.* An attempt to win a trick with a card that is not the highest in a suit by taking advantage of where the higher card(s) are placed.

*Game.* This is achieved by bidding and making a contract (or contracts) that score your side 100 points below the line.

*Grand slam.* One side making all thirteen tricks. But they will have had to *bid* seven of something as well as make it before they score the grand slam bonus – 1500 points if they are vulnerable, 1000 points if they are not.

*Guard (or stopper).* A high card in a suit protected with enough low cards to prevent the opponents running off all of the tricks in that suit.

*Honour.* An honour is any Ace, King, Queen, Jack or ten. It is not quite the same as a 'picture card' which is any Ace, King, Queen or Jack.

*Limit bid.* Any bid which tells your partner, to within a point or two, exactly how strong your hand is.

*Major suits.* Spades and Hearts, scoring 30 points below the line for each one bid and made, 30 points above the line for each one made but not bid.

*Minor suits.* Diamonds and clubs, scoring 20 points below the line for each one bid and made, 20 points above the line for each one made but not bid.

*Opening lead.* The first card to start off the play. It is always led by the player on declarer's left.

*Overtrick.* Any extra trick taken by declarer after making his contract.

*Part-score.* Any score below the line which is less than 100 points.

*Rebid.* A player who opens the bidding with one of a suit and hears a reply from partner is often expected to bid again. The next call that he makes is called his rebid.

*Redouble.* If the opponents have doubled your side, but you are completely confident of making your contract, you may redouble. This has the effect of doubling the points already at stake.

*Rubber.* Effectively the match played between the two partnerships. The rubber is won by the first side to make two games.

*Ruff.* Another word for trump. You talk about ruffing something or trumping something but, oddly enough, although you may say that you lead trumps you don't say that you lead ruffs instead.

*Side-suit.* Any of the three suits that are not trumps.

*Singleton.* Exactly one card in a suit.

*Small slam.* One side making twelve of the thirteen tricks. But they will have had to *bid* six of something as well as make it before they score the bonus – 750 points if they are vulnerable, 500 points if they are not.

*Stopper.* See Guard.

*Table.* Another way of talking about the dummy. For example, you might say 'The lead is on the table' if it is dummy's turn to start off the next trick.

*Tenace.* A combination of two cards such as A Q or K J in one hand.

*Undertrick.* When a declarer fails to make his contract, the

tricks that he is short are called undertricks.
*Void*. No cards at all in a suit.
*Vulnerable*. Having made one game. (Non-vulnerable – not having made a game.)

## BRIDGE SCORING TABLE

| **TRICK SCORE** | undoubled | doubled |
|---|---|---|
| FOR EACH ODD TRICK BID AND MADE | | |
| ♣ ◇ | 20 | 40 |
| ♡ ♠ | 30 | 60 |
| NO-TRUMP CONTRACT | | |
| FIRST ODD TRICK BID AND MADE | 40 | 80 |
| EACH ADDITIONAL ODD TRICK | 30 | 60 |

GAME TRICK SCORE OF 100 POINTS OR MORE BELOW THE LINE

| **PREMIUM SCORE** | not vulnerable undbld | not vulnerable dbld | vulnerable undbld | vulnerable dbld |
|---|---|---|---|---|
| OVERTRICKS | | | | |
| EACH OVERTRICK | TRICK VALUE | 100 | TRICK VALUE | 200 |
| SLAMS | | | | |
| SMALL SLAM BID AND MADE | 500 | | 750 | |
| GRAND SLAM BID AND MADE | 1000 | | 1500 | |

| **HONOURS** | |
|---|---|
| FOUR HONOURS IN ONE HAND | 100 |
| ALL FIVE HONOURS IN ONE HAND | 150 |
| ALL FOUR ACES IN ONE HAND AT A NO TRUMP CONTRACT | 150 |

| **RUBBERS.** | |
|---|---|
| TWO GAME RUBBER | 700 |
| THREE GAME RUBBER | 500 |
| ONE GAME IN AN UNFINISHED RUBBER | 300 |
| PARTSCORE IN AN UNFINISHED RUBBER | 50 |

| **PENALTIES** | not vulnerable undbld | not vulnerable dbld | vulnerable undbld | vulnerable dbld |
|---|---|---|---|---|
| UNDERTRICKS | | | | |
| FIRST UNDERTRICK | 50 | 100 | 100 | 200 |
| EACH ADDITIONAL UNDERTRICK | 50 | 200 | 100 | 300 |

A REDOUBLE DOUBLES THE DOUBLED VALUE